Wolfgang Amadeus Mozart

Play by Play

Wolfgang Amadeus Mozart

Play by Play

by
Alan Rich

with performances by
Alfred Brendel, piano
The Academy of
St. Martin-in-the-Fields
Sir Neville Marriner,
conductor

A Newport Classic CD/B™
Presentation

HarperCollinsSanFrancisco,
1995

Credits

Executive Producer for the Series: *Lawrence J. Kraman*

Analytical Indexing: *John Ostendorf, Rudolph Palmer, Christopher Woltmann*

Series Editor: *Jackson Braider*

Art Director: *Ann E. Kook*

Interior Design: *Stuart L. Silberman*

This recording of *Piano Concerto No. 20* was originally released on the Philips label, #420 867-2. *Piano Concerto No. 21* was originally released on the Philips label, #400 018-2.

Library of Congress Cataloging-in-Publication Data

Rich, Alan.
    Wolfgang Amadeus Mozart: Play by Play / by Alan Rich; with
    performances by Alfred Brendel, piano, The Academy of St. Martin-in-the-Fields,
    Sir Neville Marriner, conductor
    p. cm.
    "A Newport Classic CD/B presentation."
    Discography: p. 158
    Includes bibliographical references (p. 157).
    ISBN 0-06-263548-4
    ISBN 0-06-263551-4
    1. Mozart, Wolfgang Amadeus, 1756-1791. 2. Mozart, Wolfgang Amadeus, 1756-
    1791. Concertos, piano, orchestra, K. 466, D minor. 3. Mozart, Wolfgang
    Amadeus, 1756-1791. Concertos, piano, orchestra, K. 467, C major. 4. Concertos
    (Piano)—Analysis, Appreciation. I. Title

ML410.M9R55 1995 [B]   94-48625
780'.92—dc20   CIP
                                                    MN

95 96 97 98 99 ❖ RRD(C) 10 9 8 7 6 5 4 3 2 1

Contents

A Note from the Executive Producer 6

Author's Note 8

How to Use This Book.......................................10

Chapter 1 Classicism Reborn 13

Chapter 2 Music Goes Public 20

Chapter 3 Musical Structure in the Classical Era ...33

Chapter 4 Mozart: Divinity and Reality 46

Chapter 5 From Sublimity to Tragedy 56

Chapter 6 Mozart After Mozart 68

Chapter 7 Play by Play: Mozart's Reinvention
of the Piano Concerto 80

Basic Mozart: The Essential Recordings 105

Glossary 151

Further Reading and Listening 157

A Note from the Executive Producer

○

IT IS NOT WITHOUT SOME IRONY that we have chosen to call the *Play by Play* series a "CD/B" presentation. Where the race is on in computer circles to define the *next* multimedia delivery system— though the various parties involved have never actually agreed as to what the current one is—we have concocted this marriage between two very different media, invented at least one millennium and half-a-world apart. It is, as you can see, very much a *low-tech* affair: a book and a compact disc.

Mind you, we have always been very conscious of the fact that this is a new medium. It isn't just a book with a CD pasted into it for fun, nor it is a CD with a hefty set of liner notes. Each illuminates the other; each brings something to the other what it might otherwise lack, particularly as regards the exploration, the appreciation, the *understanding* of music.

I feel a bit like Cecil B. DeMille in all of this: yes, the CD/B has been ten years in the making, but the cast has certainly not been in the thousands. Clayton Carlson and Bill Crowley, of HarperCollins and PolyGram respectively, caught on very quickly, and without their enthusiastic support, it is fair to say that none of this would have happened. The people in both their organizations—James McAndrew, Leslie Clagett, Justine Davis—have all been absolutely wonderful to work with.

Somewhere along the way, classical music became *serious* music, and when that happened, many of us lost touch with the idea that this music—heavy and heady as it can be sometimes—was very often supposed to be delightful, a pleasure, a source of enlightenment. I hope that this series will open up for you what has been, up to this point, a very closed world.

LAWRENCE J. KRAMAN

Author's Note

o

As an undergraduate at Harvard, slogging my way through a pre-med major but with my heart in the Music Department, I learned to think about the listening experience as an ongoing narrative, full of thrills and surprises. The wonderful G. Wallace Woodworth would start a Haydn symphony on the 78-rpm record player, then pick up the tone arm and make us guess what was going to happen next. (We were usually wrong, but that wasn't the point.) I learned about the momentum of Beethoven's Ninth Symphony from Donald Tovey's measure-by-measure "précis" in the first volume of his *Essays in Musical Analysis* (omitted, for reasons not fathomable, in the current reprint edition of these essential musical insights). Woody in the classroom, and Tovey on paper, have shaped the way I think about listening to music over half a century. Now, however, I don't have to dash to the piano to play Tovey's musical squibs; I can hand them off, second-by-second or CD index-by-index, as clearly as if Woody were still up front running the Victrola. You can, too; that's what *Play by Play* will do for you, for me, and for music.

ALAN RICH
LOS ANGELES, 1995

How to Use
This Book

o

THE CD INCLUDED IN THIS volume has been analytically indexed. That is to say, within each track on the compact disc there has been embedded a series of inaudible codes that allows the listener to access particular moments in the composition, be it something as quick as the entry of the bass part in a fugue or something as fundamental as the start of the recapitulation section in a sonata.

The various CD player manufacturers all have developed their own particular way of accessing the index points on a compact disc and the reader should consult his or her manual for the appropriate instructions. Some older models of machines have no such capacity. However, the trick in using the sections of this book devoted to Analytical Indexing—the *Play by Play* section and the *Essential Recordings* section immediately following it—is to look at the tracking display on the CD player and relate it to what you are reading about in the book.

Here is a typical example of how the code appears in the text: [T2/i3, 1:29]. This provides the reader three pieces of information: the track (T2), the index point (i3), and the absolute time of the event in the track (1:29). What this shorthand describes, then, is the third index point on the second track of the compact disc, which occurs at 1:29 into the track. So even if your CD player doesn't have indexing, the time display will give you a precise indication of the moment a particular event being described in the text occurs.

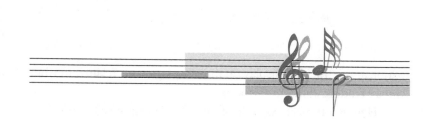

Classicism Reborn

O

"IT WAS THE BEST OF TIMES, it was the worst of times," Charles Dickens wrote at the start of *A Tale of Two Cities*, "an age of wisdom, an age of foolishness." Dickens' novel is set in the 1780s, around the time of the citizens' uprising that ushered in the French Revolution. That event served as the culmination of the new currents in mankind's view of itself and its surroundings, in the ancient political precincts of Europe and in the emerging nations of the Americas as well, that had been swirling for decades. To build further upon Dickens' contradictory pairings: it was an age of artifice, it was an age when nature was prized; an age of the rediscovery of classicism's loftiest attributes, an age when classical ideals were swept aside by the rising tide of romanticism; an age when most of the civilized world contemplated the essence of creativity: the very dualism underlying these contradictions, the dynamic balance of so much *this* versus so much *that*, was a fundamental part of the outlook of the time.

By the mid-eighteenth century, the creative spirits in the arts—and in politics as well—were obsessed with the need for change, to progress from the ideals of the recent past to a new set of definitions in every part of life. In France, the philosopher/poet (and sometime

The Parthenon: Principal temple of the Goddess Athena, on the Acropolis above Athens, this 5th century (BC) structure has come to represent the ideals of Classical art.

composer) Jean Jacques Rousseau sounded his *Retournons à la nature* in 1753—a call for a simplicity in all the arts to match the sublime logic of Nature. His call was echoed in the *Critique of Pure Reason* by German philosopher Immanuel Kant (1781) and, before that, in the writings of the young firebrand poet/dramatists Johann Wolfgang von Goethe and Johann Christoph Friedrich von Schiller. And in 1755, the German aesthetician and archeologist Johann Joachim Winckelmann published the first of several books on the art of the classical world. Using the Parthenon at Athens as the ideal of artistic integrity, he urged the readers and artists of his time to return to their cultural roots. Winckelmann's works were immensely popular and enjoyed enormous influence throughout the civilized world.

Versailles: Louis XIV's "assertion in stone of a political system." Reminiscent of classical order, Louis' grand design reflected most of all his imperialist plans for the European continent.

Johann Sebastian Bach died in 1750; George Frideric Handel, nine years later: both had become masters of the grandiose, eloquent, massive, and complex style that is now called "baroque." (The term only came into widespread use, to describe a specific artistic language, in the writings of scholars in the late nineteenth century.) By the time of their father's death, the two most talented of Bach's sons were entrenched in an entirely new musical outlook which they had both helped to formulate: music that prized simplicity over complexity—what might be referred to today as "easy listening," perhaps even as "crossover" style.

In idealizing the design of the Parthenon, even in its ruined splendor, Winckelmann's writings inspired a design trend as easily identifiable in its time as the art nouveau of the 1890s or the glass-box skyscrapers of today. As cases in point, consider the two marvelous buildings that make up the complex at Versailles, outside Paris: The great palace designed by and for Louis XIV, completed in 1685, is grand, massive, imperious, "the assertion in stone of a political system," as one critic described it. By contrast, a smaller building down the path, the Petit Trianon built in 1762 for Madame de Pompadour, mistress of Louis XV, has a pillared portico to frame and soften the shape of the structure, to balance the pomp of the larger palace. Compare, too, the twisting, straining shape of Vienna's famous Plague Memorial, its sense of frozen motion the epitome of baroque art, against the symmetry of, say, the Parliament buildings or the façade of the great Karlskirche; in both cases, the aim is obviously to welcome the observer, to soothe the eye with the serene logic of design.

Music propounds the same dichotomy. Consider the tune that begins the famous chorale setting, known everywhere as "Jesu, Joy of Man's Desiring," which occurs twice in J. S. Bach's cantata *Herz und Mund* (No. 147): a sinuous, forward-moving melody that unrolls like a spiral. Compare that with the opening of Mozart's *C-major Piano Concerto* (K. 467): two brief phrases that form a symmetrical question-and-answer unit, leading to a second, similarly constructed unit, that is rounded off with a complete cadence, before advancing to an almost exact restatement of what the listener just heard but louder and more sonorously orchestrated. Here, within a few seconds' span, is the epitome of the classical ideal, of Rousseau's naturalism and Kant's rationalism. It's not that the one kind of music is any more expressive than the other (both the Bach and the Mozart are wonderful in that regard), but they do represent two contrasting ways of shaping a musical thought.

Virtuosity

The invention of opera in seventeenth-century Italy brought to center stage the phenomenon of the virtuoso—the performer who could seize on what the composer had written and take off from there with startling new improvisations: the higher the notes, the faster the passage-work, the better. As public opera houses sprouted across the landscape, first in Italy and then north to Austria and Germany, the crowds were attracted, most of all, by the agility of leading sopranos (male and female) in sending the vocal fireworks skyward.

Violinists and keyboard players horned in on the virtuoso market; by Mozart's time, any pianist who could take a familiar tune and, on the spot, fashion an hour or so of free invention based on that tune lived like an emperor. Mozart's piano recitals, when he first came to Vienna, usually climaxed in a display of such spontaneity; later, Beethoven's improvisational powers became the stuff of legend. Treatises on the performance art carefully defined the working tools of improv: the ornaments (trills, turns, mordants, appoggiaturas, etc.) that a player could legitimately apply to the written-down music. In his performances of the slow movements in Mozart's *Concertos Nos. 20* and *21*, Alfred Brendel adds his own spare, elegant ornamentations to the simple melodic lines, very much in tune with "authentic" practice.

The best-defined battleground for virtuosos came near the end of an operatic aria or a movement of a concerto, where the orchestra came to a halt and the soloist created a cadenza from the just-heard music on the spot. Annoyed that these improvisations had come to serve more as a vehicle for the performer than the music, Mozart actually wrote out some of his own cadenzas, although not for *Concertos Nos. 20* and *21*.

Every breakthrough in the annals of human thought is at its purest at the start. The musicians who most loudly rejected the complexities of the Baroque past turned out a huge repertory of dainty but insipid pieces—"suitable for young ladies," as one publisher advertised the stuff. For every work that lingers in the memory from, say, 1756 (the year of Mozart's birth)—some of Johann Christian Bach's *Sinfoniae Concertante*, a stormy orchestral outburst by his older brother Carl Philipp Emanuel, or one of Franz Joseph Haydn's early symphonies—there were reams of merely correct exercises. Then, as in every period of artistic history, the geniuses came along. The summit of the classical style in music occurred when Haydn and Mozart, the free spirits of the age, looked carefully at the strictures of the time—the "proper" way to construct the first movement of a piano concerto, for example—and discovered their loopholes. Mozart found

Mozart's Salzburg residence: One of several homes in what is now downtown Salzburg in which all or part of the Mozart family lived. The great dome of the Salzburg Cathedral is in the background.

a way to make every **movement** of a piano **concerto** a subtle balance of predictability and surprise; Haydn did the same in his symphonies. By revealing and exploiting the ways to circumvent the rigorous rubrics of the classical style, these two geniuses helped bring the period to its end.

It's impossible to hear the slow movement of Mozart's *C-major Piano Concerto* (the one cursed with the nickname "Elvira Madigan," but more on that later) without realizing that its twenty-nine-year-old unruly genius of a composer must have been visited by a vision of an unprecedented type of musical expression, one from the future. In fact, Ludwig van Beethoven, the diabolical inventor of a new kind of music in the decade following Mozart's death, found in the Mozart concertos both a challenge and an incentive. After listening to a Mozart concerto, Beethoven expressed frustration that he "could never hope to do so well." Yet, in his **cadenzas** for Mozart's *D-minor Concerto* (K. 466), Beethoven caught the spirit of that work while also developing a common ground between the impetuous drama of Mozart's concerto and his own forceful, original musical language.

Like Johann Sebastian Bach half a century before, Mozart probed the most profound, expressive implications of the music of his time and turned them into music that brought the language of classicism in music to its glowing climax—and to its dead end. It could go no farther, not along the same path at any rate.

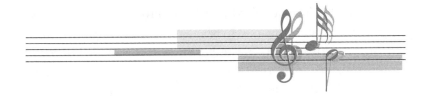

Music Goes Public

o

IF ANYTHING, J.S. BACH HAD LIVED TOO LONG and had become, in his last years, a living relic in a world he had never made. Legend has it that in May 1747, when the sixty-two-year-old Bach visited his son Carl Philipp Emanuel during Carl's stint as court composer to the Prussian monarch Frederick the Great, he tried out one of Frederick's proud, new possessions—a newfangled keyboard instrument called the *pianoforte*, whose expressive and tonal range far exceeded that of the harpsichords and clavichords of the day—and saw no future in it.

By his own standards, Bach was probably right, and the arguments persist today as to whether the *Well-Tempered Clavier* on a modern Steinway constitutes the stuff of genius or sacrilege. What the old man could not possibly perceive beyond his reaction to Frederick's new toy was the revolutionary role this instrument would play in the musical world, for composers and performers, and even more for consumers.

At the time, the idea of music consumership was a new concept. Opera houses, scattered all over Europe by 1700, had welcomed ticket-buying audiences for nearly six decades. Instrumental concert music, however, remained confined to the private halls and gardens of the nobility until around 1690, when a retired London coal-dealer named Thomas Britton invited some of the best players in the land to perform in the hayloft of his barn before an audience that subscribed at the rate of ten shillings per annum. The idea caught on; Handel and Johann Pepusch (of *Beggar's Opera* fame) were among the notables who regularly scrambled up Britton's ladder to hear and perform the latest music.

By 1730, public concerts were all the rage. Paris, Leipzig, Berlin, and Vienna erupted with rival series of chamber and orchestral concerts. With the new concert audience came a new range of tastes. After the complexity of all that uplifting music at weekly church services, the audience succumbed in its secular pursuits to a kinder, gentler music meant for easy listening. They demanded it in the concert room, and they took it home as well. The musical amateur (in the best sense, from the Latin *amare*, "to love") came into his (or her) own. This contemporary musical taste was, if anything, a two-faced monster. On the one hand, the crowds flocked to hear the latest fashionable virtuoso—especially if he happened to be a dimpled

Wunderkind like the six-year-old Wolfi Mozart. On the other hand, they hunted down a whole repertory of easy-to-play music for the family parlor, for the bourgeois equivalent of the nobleman's *musicales*, with a few friends invited over—after the dinner dishes had been cleared—for a little *Hausmusik*.

What was behind this passion for domesticated music and public virtuosi—cute or otherwise? Partly it was the emergence of a new social force in Europe, and after not very long, in America as well: the educated middle class. Spurred on by the libertarian broadsides of

The composer at age 7: Mozart was the darling of elegant society on the Continent and in England, where he was depicted in this engraving by T.Cook.

Voltaire and Rousseau and the writings on classical connoisseurship by art historian Johann Joachim Winckelmann, the populace seemed seized, almost spontaneously around 1750, with an obsession for self-improvement and knowledge.

If those were the social forces that defined cultural consumerism, there were practical considerations as well. The success of the pianoforte in eighteenth-century Europe was an explosive force that might be compared to the popularity of the compact disc today. It wasn't so much that the instrument superseded the harpsichord and clavichord in terms of tone and dynamics; it did all that—eventually, after a few false starts. More important, the pianoforte could be mass-produced, and therefore affordably priced, as harpsichords never could. By the 1780s, an Austrian family could ensconce, in the place of honor in its proudest room, a fairly reputable, locally-made piano for anywhere from 175 to 600 florins—the equivalent of $40 to $140. Measure that against Mozart's statement that he could support himself and his wife Constanze in modest circumstances for 1200 florins a year, and it works out that a piano in 1780 cost about the same percentage of a year's salary as it does today!

Inevitably, the piano in the home demanded a steady diet of new music. If the instruments could be produced cheaply, the same held true for printed sheet music. In 1755, the Leipzig firm of Breitkopf & Härtel had perfected a way of printing music using movable type, enabling cheap mass publication. The floodgates were thereby opened, and the European bourgeois household in Mozart's time became awash in music.

If the daughter of the family was the one most often granted the privilege of music lessons, virtually every composer worth his salt hastened to provide the young lady with music "easy and pleasant, for the beginner as well as the expert." The solid bourgeois composer Johann Wilhelm Hässler went so far as to audition his new sonatas before an assemblage of young ladies, begging them to "notify me of any unpleasantnesses, so that they may be altered for the benefit of my *interessées*."

And the honored Mozart? He was, of course, caught up in this onrush, as the letters and documents bear evidence. In Augsburg, in October 1777, he excitedly tried out a **sonata** on a new pianoforte with a knee-operated lever to do the job of today's damper pedal. In Paris, he saw to the publication of a *D-major Violin Sonata*, which pampers both string player and keyboardist with a double cadenza

The Piano

Early in the eighteenth century, a virtuoso named Pantaleon Hebenstreit devised an instrument based on the old-fashioned dulcimer that contained 275 strings and was played with hammers capable of rendering shades of loud and soft—a feat impossible on the harpsichord. Hebenstreit's *pantaleon* (as he modestly named it) flourished for a time; more importantly, it stimulated other inventors throughout Europe to develop instruments capable not only of tone gradations but also of cutting off notes on demand, as the pantaleon could not. The most successful of these inventors was the Florentine Bartolomeo Cristofori, whose *gravicembalo col piano e forte* ("harpsichord with loud and soft") had hinged hammers whose impact against a string could be controlled by the player. These hammers provided the player a remarkable control over loud (*forte*) and soft (*piano*) that solved the many problems found on the pantaleon. From these latter considerations Cristofori's instrument and most of its successors took their name.

The early fortepianos (a.k.a. pianofortes) underwent remarkable

in the finale. Later on, in 1785, he would raise a certain amount of hell at an unscrupulous publisher's attempt to pass off the delicious set of 1773 string quartets as being fresh from Mozart's pen. The publisher, a certain Christoph Torricella, waffled a reply. "Amateurs could never be wrongly served [by this deception]," stated the rueful Torricella, "since these too are assuredly Mozart's children."

True enough.

On 16 March 1781, the twenty-five-year-old Mozart arrived in

further developments throughout the century, mostly in the direction of controlling the hammer action so as to allow fast playing and repeated notes. By 1780, pianos still had yet to approach the qualities of today's concert grand; their range was five octaves instead of seven-plus; their sound was only slightly louder than an average harpsichord, and the notes did not sustain the way they would at Beethoven's command in his later sonatas. But the sounds were infinitely more expressive than the clangor of the harpsichord and also infinitely more controllable by the player. Few instruments have evolved as quickly as did the piano from 1720 to 1780. The slow movements of any of Mozart's mature concertos testify to how deeply he trusted the instrument to deal with the almost-vocal lines of his piano writing.

Compared to the earlier keyboard instruments, which were mostly handcrafted and expensive, the piano lent itself to mass production and, thus, affordability. For a middle-class Viennese family, owning a piano was the badge of respectability, comparable to today's projection TV.

Vienna, the city that was to be his home—where he was rich and poor, happy and miserable—for the rest of his abbreviated time on earth. His arrival was less than auspicious; as a flunky in the entourage of his Salzburg nemesis, the notorious Archbishop Colloredo, he was placed at table below the valets—galling treatment, indeed, for the composer whose ears still rang with the cheers from the premiere of *Idomeneo* in Munich two months earlier.

Vienna was not exactly unknown territory to Mozart. Nine years earlier, he had been there with his father, had heard string quartets by Haydn, and had composed his own early set of six in admiration and imitation of the older composer's *Opus 20*. His awareness of the musical swirl around him must have contributed to his chafing under the exacting Colloredo—who forbade his young minion to perform in public concerts or even to play before the Emperor. Mozart's letters home reveal a growing obsession with the idea of remaining in Vienna on his own and earning his livelihood as a private musician. Small wonder, then, that on 9 June Mozart and the Archbishop parted company, finalized, or so the story goes, with a swift kick *a posteriori* delivered to the composer by the Archbishop's chief steward, Count Arco.

Vienna, Mozart wrote, was "true Clavierland." The new instruments were to be found in every private home of substance, in the spot now occupied by today's big-screen TV. "Every girl of refinement," wrote a Viennese journalist, "must learn to play the piano…it is the easiest way to appear charming in society and thereby, if luck will have it, to make a good marriage."

To feed the pianistic passion, composers great and otherwise turned out reams of material: solo sonatas and, almost as popular, trios for piano, violin (replaceable by flute), and cello. Piano-trio versions of the orchestral repertory were immensely popular—Haydn himself, and later Beethoven, made a number of trio arrangements of their own symphonies, designed for home enjoyment. Instead of popping a compact disc of the latest Haydn symphony into the stereo, the Viennese family kept abreast of new additions to the repertory through these trio versions, which three family members might perform at home in an after-dinner *musicale.*

The piano was coming into its own in the concert rooms as well. By the time of Mozart's arrival, Viennese society was confronted with a luxurious choice of venues for partaking of the latest concert fare— and has, of course, remained so ever since. In warm weather, there was the Augarten, a splendid spot for strolling and listening; during the rest of the year, there were concerts

The harpsichord, the grand keyboard instrument of the Baroque, which produced sounds through an elaborate mechanism for plucking the strings, was already on its way out by Mozart's time, supplanted (above) by the pianoforte (or fortepiano).

in back rooms of restaurants and cafés, programs of light music at the grand Redoutensaal (part of the lordly complex of Hapsburg palaces at the edge of town), or in a redone flour warehouse, the famous Mehlgrube, and in several taverns nearby.

The Orchestra

Groups of instruments playing together dates back to the Old Testament. The idea of collecting particular instruments for a musical event, and specifying which instrument plays which music, however, only goes back to the Baroque era. Bach and Handel were among the orchestral pioneers; the scoring of Bach's *Orchestral Suite No. 4* of around 1720—three oboes, bassoon, three trumpets, timpani, strings, and continuo (a continuous bass accompaniment, played as on a harpsichord)—was the monumental rally of its time.

By 1750, orchestras were a common feature in most European cities; indeed, municipal governments and aristocrats vied with one another in the size and quality of their ensembles, with the German city of Mannheim generally regarded as the winner. The Mannheim orchestra reached its zenith under the patronage of the Elector Carl Theodor, who reigned from 1742 to 1778. Composers delighted in showing off the skills of the musicians—the instrumentation of the Bach suite plus flutes, clarinets, horns, and an enlarged string section—with all kinds of special effects: astounding crescendos, the zooming melodic style known as the "Mannheim Rocket" imitated in the last movement of Mozart's *Piano Concerto No. 20*), or the "Mannheim Sigh," the gentle dissonances in the slow movement of *No. 21*. (The Mannheim Steamroller was a much later development.) Mozart heard

Viennese concerts were varied affairs. The musician Benedikt Schwarz wrote glowingly about a "Vienna Dilettante Concert" at a tavern near the Mehlgrube sometime in the winter of 1781-82. (The term "dilettante" needs clarification here; like "amateur," its current pejora-

the Mannheim orchestra during his journey from Salzburg to Paris and wrote admiring letters about its qualities.

For the most part, the municipal orchestras played for the opera but gave concerts of their own during Lent when the theaters were closed. A typical orchestra might include three or four first and second violins and violas, two or three cellos and basses, pairs of flutes, oboes, clarinets, bassoons, horns, trumpets, and timpani, with trombones and extra percussion as needed. Typically, the conductor led from the harpsichord, sometimes from the first violinist's chair—but seldom from a podium.

Mozart's musicians for his concerto concerts were hired from Vienna's freelance pool, as they might be today. He was obviously happy with the quality of the available wind players, judging from the independent roles he allotted them in most of his mature works.

After Mozart, the orchestra continued to expand, although the harpsichord continuo became increasingly obsolete. Beethoven brought the trombone and piccolo into his *Fifth Symphony;* the contrabassoon, triangle, bass drum, and cymbals into the *Ninth*. The refinement of instrument designs—valves for the brass, an improved keying for the winds, and a bow crafted to make the strings louder—went hand in hand with the creation of larger orchestral halls. Music after Mozart is a matter of ever-increasing noise.

tive meaning was not the case in Mozart's time. If "amateur" stems from the word "to love," "dilettante" is closely related to "delight.")

Attending the Dilettante Concert, Benedikt Schwarz was captivated by "Fraulein von Auernhammer, a great dilettante on the pianoforte and Fraulein Desideria von Pauler and Mlles. Weber and Berger, who as dilettantes of singing raise much hope." Also at the concert was "Herr Mozart, Kapellmeister [who] at his incomparable pianoforte caused us to feel the sweetest enchantment."

Mozart moved freely in the circles of dilettantes. His growing fame as composer, virtuoso, and master improviser brought him several pupils, chief among them the same Josephine von Auernhammer mentioned in Schwarz's report. She became Mozart's pupil for a time in 1781—his pupil and (to his regret) his amorous pursuer as well. Alas for this dilettante, her physical endowments weren't the match of her musicianship. "She is as fat as a farm-wench," Mozart wrote, "perspires so that you feel inclined to vomit ... so loathsome, dirty and horrible. Faugh!"

Of all the entertainments devised for Viennese concert life in the last quarter of the eighteenth century, none loomed larger than the concerto for the pianoforte, in dialogue with an ensemble of strings, a few winds, perhaps even a brass instrument or two. Clavierland was awash in clavier concertos. Among Vienna's ensconced composers, Georg Christoph Wagenseil (1715-1777) turned out no fewer than sixty concertos for the keyboard; Johann Albrechtsberger (1736-1809)

A corner in the Mozart museum, in his Salzburg birthplace, with one of the composer's own keyboard instruments.

and Carl Ditters von Dittersdorf (1739-99) followed close behind. Mozart soon caught the bug, and in December 1782—his fame now nailed down by the success of the *Abduction from the Seraglio*—he himself published and advertised his first three Viennese concertos. The concertos, he wrote,

in a command of media today's press agents might envy, "are a happy medium between what is too easy and too difficult; they are very brilliant, pleasing to the ear and natural, without being vapid."

It would be some months yet before Mozart would begin the series of piano concertos *(Nos. 15-25)*, offered in public subscription concerts for which he himself served as impresario, that stand as one of music's authentic miracles. Meanwhile, he participated avidly in Vienna's frantic and fruitful musical life. He overcame his revulsion of the fat Fraulein Auernhammer enough to take part in concerts at the home of the lady's rich father. He officiated at the piano as his songs were sung in cafe concerts and at lodge meetings. ("Agreeable and instructive occupation...songs with music by the celebrated Mozart" ran a 1788 advertisement.)

He played **chamber music** at house parties, in ensembles that might also include Haydn, Dittersdorf, and the Bohemian-born Johann Baptist Vanhal. It was at one of these parties that Haydn took the visiting Leopold Mozart aside to deliver his famous paean of praise ("Before God and as an honest man, I tell you that your son is the greatest composer known to me..."). To reward this esteem, Mozart dedicated six superlative string quartets to Haydn and rejoiced to see them published and widely circulated, as few of his major works had been at that time.

Vienna's musical life did not, therefore, actually spurn the importuning of the man-child from Salzburg, as it would its own native Franz Schubert a few decades later. For a few glorious years, at least, the city and its most cherishable musician contributed handsomely to each other's luster.

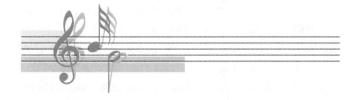

Musical Structure in the Classical Era

ARCHITECTURE, WROTE THE GREAT POET of the Enlightenment Johann Wolfgang von Goethe, is frozen music. True, he lifted the line from Friedrich Wilhelm Joseph von Schelling, a minor contemporary philosopher; still, the observation is keen and to the point. The ideals that drove the eighteenth-century builders to re-create in stone and masonry the shapes and structural ideals of ancient Athens and Rome were clearly mirrored in the forces that drove the eighteenth-century composers as well.

Why all this concern about musical structure, with all the daunting vocabulary it brings with it: sonata form, rondo, development, recapitulation, variations? In romantic films, all a composer had to do was to create a pretty tune or two (usually, it turned out to be by Russian composer Sergei Rachmaninoff), and before long they would be played in Carnegie Hall by a full symphony orchestra.

Nobody stood over the matinee-idol genius to make sure his opening theme modulated correctly into the second theme, or that the recapitulation returned to the original key; after all, music, in the view of the Movieland popularizers, exists only for its tunes.

It would be wrong to deny this completely, of course; music does, indeed, depend on the attractiveness of its material. But the power in that music, its sweep as it moves through time, comes not only from the pretty tunes, but also from their progress, how their comings and goings become the essence of the listener's perception of structure and logic. The architectural analogy holds true, of course: The structural integrity of, say, the Parthenon is easily sensed, because of the thrilling symmetry of its design, the perspective in its overall planning; divorced from this structural integrity, the materials of the Parthenon—piled up as a mound of pillars, carved sculptures, or masonry blocks—would never have such an impact.

By the same token, it is also thrilling when enlightened architects break out of the design norm and create something purposely and dramatically askew. A stupendous example, dating back to long before the revival of classicism, handsomely demonstrates the virtues of freedom in artistic form: The cathedral at Chartres, with its pair of great steeples of totally different design, seems, at first glance, like some kind of structural incompetence, perhaps, until a couple important facts are noted. First, that the architects of the steeples worked four centuries apart and incorporated the design ideals of two different historical eras into their work. It never would have occurred to the sixteenth-century builders of the north tower, the "Clocher Neuf," to copy the design of the twelfth-century "Clocher Vieux" just for the sake of symmetry; artists in those times worked true to the spirit of their own era. The idea of the historical architect—Thomas Jefferson designing his Monticello along the lines of a Greek temple, for example, or a fast-food joint built to resemble the Leaning Tower of Pisa—only came into being many centuries after the creation of Nôtre-Dame de Chartres. Second, both architects designed their respective steeples in marvelous proportion to the rest of the building. The balance that eventually resulted, somewhere between violation and integrity, is, in a word, sublime.

In similar fashion, Mozart violates the "rules" of classical form by bringing the main theme back in the wrong key, or by reprising all his themes in a different order from the way they were before. Of course, Mozart never worked from a rule book. The intellectual climate of his time suggested certain affinities between music and the other arts, and he had the genius to seek out

Monticello: Thomas Jefferson's home in Virginia, which he himself designed under the influence of the Classical revival.

ways of infusing those affinities into his creations. The actual laws of classical form, as they are taught today, were formulated by scholars long after Mozart and Haydn were gone, and after the rebellious Beethoven turned some of these principles upside down in his own music. The nineteenth-century musicologists examined the thousands of symphonies, concertos, sonatas, and chamber works that had survived from the previous century, observed certain shared tendencies in these works, and formulated the outlines for the various kinds of musical form that are still studied today.

Musical structure is the interaction between the listener's memory and the time a piece of music occupies. The listener hears a tune at the start of a work, then becomes aware of the shape of the melody, the rhythmic relationship of its notes, the tone color of the instruments playing it. All of these form the most recognizable aspects of that tune, and they remain in the memory. Other, more subtle qualities also contribute to the memory of the tune—most of all, its **harmony**. Even if the listener doesn't have perfect pitch, the key of the work (also called the **tonality**) is an important facet of one's awareness. With Mozart, certain kinds of melody demand the identity of a specific key, if for no other reason than the fact that the instruments he wants to use are more comfortable in that key. C major was, for the eighteenth-century orchestra, the key of trumpets, drums, and bright military-style flourishes and fanfares, which is what is heard at the start of the *C-major Piano Concerto No. 21* (and the *Jupiter*

Symphony, and the later *Piano Concerto No. 25*). E-flat is a happy key for woodwinds, especially the clarinet, as well as for horns, and these instruments are wonderfully used to create the warm, caressing tone color of the *Piano Concerto No. 22* and the *Symphony No. 39*. And so, tonality is one of the elements that contribute to one's memory of a work and will aid the recognition of that material when, in the course of the composition, it returns.

The composer's next task is to introduce the element of contrast, which can be achieved in many ways. The original theme can become the basis for a set of variations, each successive section preserving the outline of the original theme but adding details, changing the mood, turning an initially sad tune into a triumphal march (and back again); the last movement of the *Piano Concerto No. 24* is a splendid example of this. Or the composer may move from the initial theme into totally new regions. Where the opening had a certain stability—recognizable tune, scoring, tonality—it would not do just to repeat what's already been heard again and again. (Even in today's musical style known not quite accurately as "minimalism," the real point isn't merely to repeat a theme *verbatim* and *ad infinitum*, but to introduce tiny, subtle shifts that become big and dramatic within the repetitive context.)

It's easy enough for the composer to start a piece in one place and then to end it somewhere else; that certainly takes care of the need for contrast. The slow movement of the *Concerto No. 20* is a case in point: it begins with a gentle, melting theme, in the key of B-flat, beautifully treated by both piano and orchestra. Then Mozart moves on by introducing another theme, still in B-flat, but nicely contrasting in melodic outline and scoring. Then the initial theme

Mozart by the Numbers

"Symphony No. 41," "Symphony No. 5," "K. 551"—what do these numbers mean? Consider a familiar Mozart score, the *Jupiter* Symphony, as a case in point. According to the Vienna firm of Breitkopf und Härtel, which first published most of Mozart's orchestral works in the early nineteenth century, this is *No. 41* in the chronological order of symphonies, although that enumeration leaves out several orchestral pieces that Mozart assembled from his other works and called "symphonies." The *Jupiter* is also "No. 1," however, in the set of symphonies arranged as piano duets and published by C. F. Peters in Leipzig around 1830. In the Köchel catalog, it appears as "K.

551." Mozart had nothing to do with the name *Jupiter,* although it's a good description of the music; it was coined by the London impresario J. P. Salomon, the same man who sponsored the London concerts by Franz Joseph Haydn. The name first appeared in print in 1823, in a solo piano version by Muzio Clementi.

In the days before music publishing became a flourishing industry, many great works survived only in manuscript, and exact identification and dating was almost impossible. In 1862, the Austrian botanist, mineralogist, and musical enthusiast Ludwig von Köchel (1800-1877) published his *Thematic and Chronological Index of the Works of Mozart,* a labor of love that had occupied him for decades: hunting down every scrap of Mozart he could find, estab-

returns; it's a simple, straightforward arrangement—ABA—so far. But then, the ear is jerked into a violently contrasting section: a new theme in a different tonality (G minor, a close relative of B-flat), and a different scoring. Then the theme returns to A, and the music flows

lishing the date of composition by any number of sleuthing techniques, and assigning numbers to each score in turn. Its last number, 626, went to the *Requiem,* left unfinished by Mozart at his death. Considering the number of works still undiscovered in his day, and the number erroneously attributed to Mozart but now properly identified, Köchel made relatively few mistakes. Others in recent times have revised his numberings, but his original list was so widely circulated and prized at the time, and so close to being authoritative, that few scholars bother with the revisions.

Thus, the letter "K" (or sometimes "K. V." for *Köchel Verzeichnis* or "Köchel Catalogue") and a number following a Mozart work is a fair identification. It indicates, for example, that the *Piano Concerto No. 20* (K. 466) comes from approximately the same period as the so-called *Dissonant Quartet* (K. 465) and the remarkably dramatic *C-minor Piano Sonata* (K. 457) and not long before *The Marriage of Figaro* (K. 496). Other composers have benefited from Köchel's example: the "S" designation appended to a Bach work indicates its place in Wolfgang von Schmieder's catalog; the "D" postscript in Schubert's catalog shows the hand of the distinguished scholar Otto Erich Deutsch. From Beethoven's time on, most well-regarded composers had easier access to publication as they completed one score after another, and the composers themselves assigned *Opus* ("work") numbers to their music as they wrote.

Salzburg: The handsome Austrian city on the Salzach, a Celtic settlement and then Roman, was since the Renaissance a gathering place for the arts; today its architecture and civic layout remain pretty much as they were in the time of its great native son, Mozart.

on to a serene close: ABACA, in other words. The outline couldn't be simpler, but it serves the music very well, providing unity, contrast, clarity, and surprise. Call this the "rondo;" its name comes from a very old poetic form, the rondeau, which had a repeated refrain between the new verses.

Out of these relatively simple, "closed" forms emerged a more complex kind of musical arrangement, supple and sublimely logical. Its most common name, among today's scholars, is **sonata form**; it could just as easily be called "symphony form" or "string quartet form," since it didn't depend on whether the work in question was a solo sonata, or a chamber or orchestral work. It evolved as a way of arranging the substance of a movement in any kind of instrumental music, and it served composers as a manner of arrangement capable of infinite variety. One point, however, bears reiteration: no composer in the eighteenth century, or later, ever worked from a sonata-form chart pinned to a worktable. The predominance of this kind of arrangement stemmed from its intrinsic and exquisite logic, its extreme utility and flexibility in serving the musical language of its time. It is usually the form of the first movement of a symphony or concerto, because that is customarily the longest and most complex of the three or four that make up the entire work; there's no reason, however, why it couldn't also serve for any of the ensuing movements—the slow movement of Mozart's *Jupiter* Symphony, for example.

The three basic sections of sonata form derive their personalities mostly from the arrangement of tonality. The first section—the **exposition**—presents the material in the original key and then, through a transition, introduces contrasting material in a second key usually closely related to the first (G to C, for example). Typically, along the way from the first to the second main section, the composer devises ways to undermine the stability of the harmony, to disrupt the even flow of the initial **melody**; out of this unsettledness, a new stability will eventually emerge. Most important, the composer will have brought the music to a different key area, one related to the initial key but not quite the same. Key "relationships" occur when two keys share most of the same notes. The difference between C major (the opening tonality of *Piano Concerto No. 21*) and G major (the key of the second principal theme), for example, is a single note—F-natural in C and F-sharp in G—so Mozart can get from C to G through a simple transition. (But even here, he throws in a monkey wrench; along the way from C to G, he pauses momentarily in the unexpected key of G *minor*. He then climbs out, of course, and continues on the expected path.)

After a more or less definitive close (often with the indication that the entire exposition is to be repeated), the second section—the **development**—contrasts with the exposition primarily in its tendency to zoom through a number of keys. Sometimes it draws upon material from the exposition (as in the first movement of the *Concerto No. 20*); other times it introduces new ideas (as in *No. 21*). Overall, its main distinction is its trajectory across many areas of harmonic instability and, at its end, a building of expectation for the **recapitulation,** which returns to the material from the exposition, but in the original key. The purpose here is to round off the movement with a sense of consistency; sometimes the composer introduces a bit of sleight of hand so that the music remains in its tonic key without sounding repetitious. Mozart is a delightful trickster in this regard; in the recapitulations of the first movements of both *Concertos Nos. 20* and *21*, he brings back some of his material in a different order than originally heard, leaves out some altogether, and generally teases the audience out of its expectations. (In the "Play by Play" analyses of these works, there are letter diagrams to represent the sequence of events in these two complex movements.)

Beyond the basic structure of sonata form, certain added features may occur: an introduction (usually slow, often majestic and suspenseful) before the start of a symphonic movement, for example, or an extra final passage (called a **coda**) at the end. Additionally, two features are peculiar to the concerto. An opening **ritornello** introduces some, or occasionally all, of the themes of the movement, but all in the same key. The purpose here, which points to the close relation between concerto and **opera**, is, of course, to delay and thus dramatize the soloist's entrance. Sometimes the soloist is granted a sort of "bow" before getting on with the movement; the short digression at the entrance in the *Concerto No. 21* is an illustration of this.

Near the end of the movement, however, the soloist really gets to monopolize the spotlight. The orchestra comes to a halt, while the soloist engages in a **cadenza**, a virtuosic improvisation on the material of the movement (or, in extreme cases, on anything else the soloist may have in mind). Mozart, of course, improvised his own cadenzas for the concertos he performed, and some of them were later written down and have survived. His

Young Mozart: An idealized portrait of the composer rendered by M. Rodig.

cadenzas for the 20th and 21st concertos did not survive. Ludwig van Beethoven's cadenzas for *No. 20* are extraordinary tributes by a younger composer to the surging drama in Mozart's work. (Alfred Brendel uses a cadenza of his own devising in this recording of *No. 20,* and one by Rado Lupu in *No. 21.*)

The musical ideals of Haydn and Mozart, their genius at concocting melodies of consummate clarity and originality, and their extraordinary command of harmonic coloration, seemed to mesh perfectly with the spirit of classical structure. Later in musical history, composers seemed anxious to blur these clear outlines and to work toward a more continuous, seamless kind of music in which the integrity of classical form, particularly its emphasis on the balance of elements and symmetry, was less important.

Even Mozart seemed to delight in stretching the "rules" of the time, and it's safe to say of his mature works that no two obey those rules in exactly the same way. In one early piano concerto (*No. 9*), he allows his soloist a premature entry long before the stipulated juncture. In the sublime slow movement of *No. 21,* he totally blurs the point of recapitulation; the main theme slides in, in the "wrong" key.

Does it matter? Or does the problem at hand involve maintaining so even a musical flow that a listener might forget to take a breath? The musical spirit of the eighteenth century makes a fascinating and orderly study, because of the abundance of "correct" music for which practical descriptions and conclusions are easily arrived at. It is an equally intriguing study, however, because of the many different ways the true geniuses of the time found of composing "incorrectly" and, therefore, brilliantly.

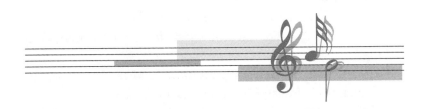

Mozart: Divinity and Reality

o

Before God and as an honest man, I tell you that your son is the
greatest composer known to me in person or by reputation.
                    —Franz Joseph Haydn to Leopold Mozart, 1785

AT THE TIME OF WOLFGANG AMADEUS MOZART'S arrival in
Vienna, Franz Joseph Haydn was one of the few musical figures
of importance who had had no difficulty in recognizing the awesome, spontaneous genius of the mercurial young Salzburger.
When Haydn's stunning repertory of string quartets was circu-
lating in Vienna, where it was performed in the homes of the
music-loving aristocracy, the audience often included the divinely
inspired, younger musician, whose rightful share of honor and
fame would come more slowly and then only sporadically.

Inspired by the marvelous textures and the structural freedoms in Haydn's compositions, Mozart dedicated a set of his own string quartets to the older composer. It was at a performance of one of those works in Vienna that Haydn spoke his famous words to Mozart's proud father, Leopold, during the final decade of Mozart's tragically brief life, a decade marked by bursts of both glory and desperation. At twenty-nine, Mozart had already produced more great music—and suffered more hardships—than most composers do in a long lifetime.

His beginnings were certainly auspicious. Leopold Mozart was a composer at the court of Salzburg, the storybook town in central Austria which—give or take a neon sign or two—could still pass today for the burg where, on 27 January 1756, Wolfgang Amadeus Mozart was born to Leopold and his wife, Maria Anna. Leopold wasn't much of a composer; the one piece of his that is still performed today is a jolly number called *A Musical Sleighride*, which blends the jangle of toy instruments into the strings of a chamber orchestra. (For a long time, the *Sleighride* was attributed to Haydn, under the title *Toy Symphony*. Scholars have since straightened out the matter of credit.) Leopold was more famous as a

Leopold Mozart: Father of Wolfgang, himself renowned as a violin virtuoso and teacher.

teacher than as a composer, and his treatise on violin-playing is still worth consulting, if only because it crystallizes a performer's outlook around 1750.

Once Leopold realized what he had on his hands—an infant prodigy who at the age of three already evinced an amazing gift for picking out tunes of his own at the keyboard and memorizing the tunes of others after hearing them but once—he abandoned his own career and devoted himself to managing Wolfgang's. In January 1762, the six-year-old periwigged cherub astounded the court at Munich by playing the violin with his older sister Nannerl—a talent in her own right—at the keyboard. In Vienna, the Mozart moppets completely overwhelmed the formidable Empress Maria Theresa and her court; the story goes that Wolfgang climbed up onto the Empress' lap and proposed to the young princess Marie Antoinette.

A year later, Leopold Mozart bundled up his two accomplished offspring and set out on a tour that would, in three years, take them across Europe and to London; they were greeted everywhere by cheering audiences. The advertisements that survive from that journey suggest more of a circus atmosphere than a musical event: "he will play the harpsichord with the keyboard covered with a cloth...he will instantly name all notes played at a distance...he will improvise as long as may be desired, and in any key." Small wonder, then, that Wolfgang made his tortuous way toward maturity with the awkwardness of a showbiz kid. By the time he reached sixteen, he had spent half his life as a roadshow freak.

Some of these travels produced more important results than merely showcasing a gifted child, however. In London, the eight-year-old Mozart won the admiration and friendship of Johann Christian Bach, the youngest and most musically successful son of Johann Sebastian. From the young Bach's works, Mozart absorbed an Italianate elegance and charm that soon showed up in his own music.

Johann Christian Bach (1735-1782): Youngest of J.S. Bach's composer sons and, during his lifetime, the most widely famed. In London he began one of the world's first public concert series. He befriended the child Mozart on the young prodigy's first visit to London and probably influenced his style as well.

Until his later years in Vienna, and his friendship with Haydn, Mozart looked to Christian Bach as his most congenial outside influence.

Starting in 1769, Leopold took the teenage Wolfgang on several trips to Italy. There, the boy could absorb that country's musical language first-hand, particularly the Italians' way of devising melodies through which the human voice could break listeners' hearts. In Rome, he heard the famous church motet, *Miserere*, by Gregorio Allegri, from the late Baroque era, which—for reasons not entirely clear —the Vatican had pronounced super-sacred and forbidden to be published. True to form, Mozart came away from a performance, took some manuscript paper, and reproduced the entire score from memory. Not at all miffed, the Pope awarded the thirteen-year-old genius his Order of the Golden Spur.

Mozart's excursions, however, did more than merely mine gold for the family purse. The extraordinary powers of perception that enabled him to exercise his legendary feats of memory also served him in a broader sense. Wherever he traveled, he listened and absorbed styles and techniques that he then synthesized into his own

Mozart on the Road

From his emergence as a baby prodigy until his sixteenth year, Mozart spent half his life on the road, with a total of four of his thirty-five years spent in a stage-coach. Imagine being wedged in among eight or more fellow-passengers, traversing the 800 miles between Salzburg and Paris, or the 200 between Vienna and Prague, plodding at ten miles an hour over unpaved roads, through mountain passes, staying at whatever inns might be along the way.

It's hard to track down the exact details of Mozart's travels, where he stopped or how long a particular journey lasted. But one precious book, which, alas, nobody reads anymore, gives some idea of what travel might have been like in central Europe in 1787. Eduard Mörike, a Suabian ex-pastor whose poems were turned into songs by Schumann and Brahms, wrote a brief novel called *Mozart on the Way to Prague* that was published in 1855. Throughout his life, Mörike was obsessed with the desire to "live into" Mozart's life; in this book of 124 pages, he suc-

musical language: the Handelian grandiosity in London along with the intimate charm of J. C. Bach's music; the warmth of Italy; the virtuosity in the orchestras of Germany; the elegance in the sounds of French woodwinds. By the age of sixteen, he had created a prodigious legacy, amounting to more than 150 separate entries in the Köchel chronological catalogue of his works: operas, oratorios, and other large-scale choral compositions; twenty symphonies and a plenitude of more casual orchestral works; chamber music, keyboard solos, and a large repertory for violin and keyboard for his frequent appearances

ceeds, riding with the composer in the coach from Vienna to Prague. The year is 1787: *Figaro* has been a mild success in Vienna but a huge triumph in Prague; now the Mozarts are on their way to attend the premiere of *Don Giovanni,* which Prague has commissioned. The story is fantasy, yet, somehow it portrays Mozart and Constanze as a very real couple undergoing the very real rigors of eighteenth-century travel. They stop in a village where Mozart wanders into the garden of a local magnate and absent-mindedly picks an orange from a prized tree. Instead of cas-tigating him, however, the tycoon welcomes Mozart, and he comes away with a tune that he will use in the new opera. He plays the grim finale of *Don Giovanni* for the assembled guests; they are disturbed by it but recognize the genius of its creator. Entirely Mörike's invention, the vignette is charmingly, if garrulously, detailed. Any ardent Mozartian holds it as a most cherished piece of literature.

with Nannerl. Some of this music is, to be sure, merely the work of a clever observer and imitator of other people's styles. More to the point, however: a lot of it isn't. In the tender tune during the slow movement of the symphony *No. 20,* which could pass for Susanna's music in *The Marriage of Figaro* fourteen years later, for example, the voice of this supremely endowed adolescent can wring the heart.

No matter how rewarding the travels were, however, home for Mozart was in Salzburg, the ancient Catholic stronghold where the power of the Archbishop was both political and spiritual—and mighty in both regards. A job in the retinue of Archbishop/Prince Hieronymus von Colloredo was the only game in town for a musician. Whereas Leopold Mozart had obsequiously succumbed to the royal thumbscrew, his son was not that willing. Wolfgang suffered constantly in the position of court concertmaster, turning out a continual repertory of church pieces and little else, entertaining the Archbishop's guests with his concertos and serenades. At sixteen, his name had already gotten around, and commissions had begun to arrive: an opera for Milan, another for Munich. The Archbishop tended to raise a ruckus at the frequent departures of his young genius to tend to his out-of-town performances. "If I were offered a salary of 2,000 gulden by the Archbishop of Salzburg," Mozart wrote, "and only 1,000 gulden somewhere else, I should take the second offer. Instead of the extra 1,000 gulden I should enjoy good health and peace of mind."

In 1777, the twenty-one-year-old Mozart determined to improve his status. He set off for Paris to find more enlightened employment and delighted the Parisians with a number of splendid works, including a symphony (*No. 31*) full of original and entertaining orchestral tricks. His mother had come along, even though she had not been well back in Salzburg, and in July 1778 she died, a stranger in a strange land. Subsequently, sorrow and disappointment dogged the Paris venture; early in 1779, Mozart headed back to Salzburg. On the way, he stopped in Mannheim, whose splendid court orchestra was an object of pilgrimage for all European musicians. In

Mozart's birthplace: On one of Salzburg's busiest downtown streets, the home is now a shrine, housing a small Mozart museum and several of the instruments on which he composed and played.

Mannheim, too, he visited the Weber family; he had known them before and had once openly courted Aloysia, the prettiest and most musical of the four Weber daughters. Now, however, he found Aloysia married to someone else: another weight to add to the sorrows of the Paris expedition.

It is always risky to try to link events in an artist's life to specific artworks; history's muse stands ready to contradict these easy connections—with the joyous assertiveness in the works of Franz Schubert's illness-racked final months, or the youthful vigor in the eighty-one-year-old Giuseppe Verdi's *Falstaff*. Yet there is a new range of expressiveness that seems to have entered Mozart's music after his return to Salzburg. It can be heard in the *Sinfonia Concertante for Violin and Viola*, especially in the slow movement, where the soloists seem to converse like lovers in the twilight. Those same lovers (or their close relatives) seem to be conversing in a lighter, but no less sincere, vein in the *Concerto for Two Pianos*. And the audience's collective breath is suspended time and again in the opera *Idomeneo*, composed in 1780 for Munich; here, within the framework of the old-fashioned *opera seria* that had flourished and withered for over a century, Mozart found the means to endow his stock-figure characters with a sense of humanness, arrived at through the sheer beauty of his rich vocal writing.

Idomeneo was, for Mozart, the greatest triumph of his life so far; it endowed him with world stature, no longer as an enchanted child, but as a twenty-four-year-old mature genius. It was also, however, the breaking point between Mozart and his native Salzburg. Early in 1781, Colloredo summoned the wayward composer to his apartments in Vienna, where the princely entourage was visiting, and ordered Mozart to give up this wandering lifestyle and knuckle down to the lackeyhood that was his proper place. When Mozart tried to protest, one of Colloredo's other lackeys, a certain Count

Arco, unceremoniously booted him down the stairs. Mozart described the scene in a series of letters to his father. In the same letters, he asserted and reasserted his determination to forsake Salzburg forever and lay siege to Vienna, the world's musical capital. True to his word, he never again saw the city of his birth.

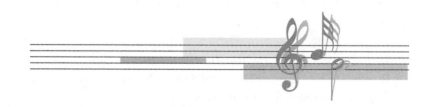

CHAPTER 5

From Sublimity to Tragedy

o

I was suddenly frightened. It seemed to me that I had heard a voice of God.

    —Antonio Salieri, in Peter Shaffer's *Amadeus*, on hearing the slow movement from Mozart's *Serenade for Thirteen Winds in B-flat major*

LIFE AS A FREELANCE COMPOSER was no easier in Vienna in 1781 than it is in New York or Hollywood today. Mozart's time in Paris had already shown him the depressing prospect of trying to peddle one's wares door to door. Simply because it was the center of the musical world, teeming with musical hopefuls on every street corner, Vienna would be worse. Yet Mozart knew that he had within him the power to offer Vienna the greatest music it had ever heard and that he had no choice but to remain there.

His friends, the Webers, had moved to Vienna from Mannheim and welcomed Mozart as a houseguest. Fridolin Weber had died in 1779 during the family move; his daughter Aloysia, once the apple of Mozart's eye, was now happily married and ensconced in a brilliant singing career. The widow Weber instituted a campaign to direct Mozart's attention toward a younger, less pretty daughter, Constanze. Wolfgang was willingly persuaded, and he and Constanze were married in August 1782. Leopold Mozart bestowed a grudging blessing; he had always regarded the Weber brood as unworthy of the Mozart name. Furthermore, Leopold had never approved of Wolfgang's break with the Archbishop; relations between father and son would never return to their former warmth.

Wolfgang and Constanze settled into one of the world's less promising marriages. For one thing, neither was much to look at: she was plain of face and dowdy; he, diminutive and pudgy, with a squashed nose and protruding eyes that not even the most romanticized portraits could conceal. According to observers, he was so fidgety that Constanze had to cut up his food for him, fearing that he might lose a finger. Much is made of Mozart's letter-writing—to Constanze, to younger relatives, to virtually everyone except Leopold. Peter Shaffer's *Amadeus* (both the play and the movie) deals, at inordinate length, with the seeming contradiction between the language of these letters and the sublimity of Mozart's music. One refutation is, however, that this was the language of the time, indulged in by the highbrow and the lowbrow alike. A play that was wildly popular in Vienna, Goethe's *Götz von Berlichen,* contained an anatomical invitation so vivid that Austrians in Mozart's time, and today as well, need only shout "Götz" to an opponent to score points in an argument. Another refutation is that these letters by Mozart, published many times over, also constitute some of the most poignant documents on the struggles of a composer making his way in the musical world and attempting to balance the conflicts within a personal world as well.

Mozart's admission into Viennese society was brilliantly heralded by a comic opera, the *Abduction from the Seraglio,* that became an immediate sensation. It had everything going for it: a plot set in the storybook Middle East, complete with a despotic pasha, a heroine held captive, a rescuing hero, and a gathering of comic characters; a German text with spoken dialogue; and an orchestra full of exotic percussion. It premiered on 16 July 1782, two weeks before Mozart's marriage. The opera's heroine was also named Constanze.

Antonio Salieri: Highly regarded composer at the Austrian court in Mozart's time; in later years, a respected teacher of both Beethoven and Schubert.

Seraglio earned Mozart entry into the court of Joseph II, emperor of the Holy Roman Empire, who was something of a self-proclaimed opera connoisseur (although he did grumble that the opera contained "too many notes"). As depicted (more accurately than not) in *Amadeus*, Joseph surrounded himself with a cabal of musicians, each ready at a moment's notice to bite off the head of the next. Antonio Salieri was, without a doubt, the most talented of these; his surviving legacy of operas, concertos, religious music, and chamber works displays a certain mastery of a predictable classical style. Also at the court was the gadfly author, poet, *bon vivant*, and political machinator Lorenzo da Ponte, whose life would end many years later as a bookseller and teacher of Italian in New York City. Da Ponte and Mozart hit it off in a series of operatic collaborations, only partially successful with Vienna's rather frivolous operatic crowd, that stand today among the world's imperishable masterworks: *The Marriage of Figaro* in 1786, *Don Giovanni* a year later, and *Così fan tutte* two years after that.

As he became renowned, at least among Vienna's more enlightened music-lovers, for the sublimity of his operas, Mozart was simultaneously proving himself as a piano virtuoso, supported by a series of concertos which he himself introduced at subscription concerts. It is important to consider these piano concertos and the operas together, since they stem from a single impulse: to touch and break hearts through the sheer beauty of melody (colored with a harmonic language richer than anyone had previously attempted), tone color, and virtuosity employed not for empty display but for dramatic expression. The heroes and heroines of Mozart's operas became the protagonists of the piano concertos as well—not literally, perhaps, but certainly in spirit. The first and last movements of the *Concerto No. 20* are full of the thrusts of Don Giovanni's sword; the haunting "one-finger" melody in the slow movement has the naive ecstasy of *Figaro*'s Cherubino; the outburst of jollity that ends the concerto, after the arguments have subsided, could be the finale of *Figaro*, with the songs of forgiveness that clear the air. And the haunting nocturne that draws tears in the slow movement of *No. 21* is the melancholy of the abandoned Countess in that opera, just as her first **aria**, "Porgi, amor," could be one of the ravishing dialogues between piano and winds in any of the mature concertos.

By 1786, the Mozarts were as well off as they would ever be. If *Figaro* proved too sophisticated for the Viennese, it was enormously successful in not-too-distant Prague, apparently a city that recognized the importance of supporting new music. From Prague came a commission for the next opera, *Don Giovanni*, produced with even greater acclaim—and similarly misunderstood back in Vienna, where Mozart was obliged to add a new slapstick scene to placate the locals. "The opera is heavenly," Emperor Joseph told Mozart, "but no food for the teeth of my Viennese."

The piano concerto concerts provided plenty of sustenance, however, for the teeth of the audiences and for the composer himself. Mozart could always be counted upon to put on a good show, dashing through the concertos with spectacular aplomb, engaging in spontaneous improvisational displays for an adoring audience. The great Haydn, certainly the most widely acclaimed composer of his time, befriended Mozart and did what he could to intercede for jobs and commissions. Hearing concerts of Haydn's string quartets in some of Vienna's aristocratic palaces had inspired Mozart to compose six of his own between 1782 and 1785, which he dedicated to the older composer. "A father who had decided to send his sons out into the great world," the dedication began, "thought it his duty to entrust them to the protection and guidance of a man who...happened to be his best friend." It was after a per-

formance of three of these works, with Leopold in attendance and Wolfgang and Haydn among the players, that Haydn took the elder Mozart aside to assure him that "Before God and as an honest man, I tell you that your son is the greatest composer known to me in person or by reputation...".

Yet life for the young couple was hardly a bed of roses. Totally spoiled in his early *Wunderkind* days, Wolfgang had never learned the proper respect for money; the greater his income, as he saw it, the more cash to fritter away on

Mozart at Vienna: Another idealized, after-the-fact portrait (by O. Pelton); it shows Mozart playing his Don Giovanni *before a gathering of "lords and artists."*

drink, billiards, and possibly gambling as well. Constanze had fallen victim to a series of chronic ailments and spent a great deal of her time, and the family money, at expensive spas. Meanwhile, the Emperor Joseph had gotten into an expensive war with Turkey, and that meant reduced patronage for the arts at home.

When Mozart returned from Prague at the end of 1787, after the spectacular triumph of *Don Giovanni*, he was offered the job of Court Chamber-Musician, but at a salary less than half of what his predecessor had earned. The extra income did little to ease his finan-

The Scene

Vienna in Mozart's time was honeycombed with music. The well-heeled flocked to the spacious Burgtheater, located just at the edge of the imperial complex of palaces. By today's standards, this grandest of all Viennese theaters was diminutive, seating perhaps 400—at gala concerts, with the imperial orchestral forces increased to, perhaps, 100 players, there must have been a lot of sound indeed. Less formal concerts were held regularly at the Augarten, built in 1775 by Joseph II as part of a grand public park on the island between the Danube and the Danube Canal, or at the Mehlgrube, an ancient flour warehouse in which a concert hall had recently been built.

Opera also flourished at the Burgtheater, where tickets were prohibitively priced but sold quickly nonetheless; lighter, more intimate fare was presented in smaller venues, including the tumble-down house at the edge of town where Mozart and Emanuel Schikaneder staged their *Magic*

cial situation, obliging him to fill his time grinding out dance music for court balls. Although invitations for public performances had begun to dwindle, he continued to compose his own music whenever he could, in the hope of publication—which sometimes materialized and sometimes didn't. In the months after Prague, he produced an extraordinary legacy that included the two string quintets in C major and G minor—in which deep suffering lurks beneath the surface— and the three last symphonies, exuberant and majestic, which the composer never heard.

Flute before an audience weaned on folk plays and the eighteenth-century Viennese equivalent of burlesque.

Chamber music, the most aristocratic of the musical fare, thrived in the palaces of families with the familiar names of Lobkowitz, Lichnowsky, and Razumovsky. It was in such luxe surroundings that a quartet of players might include both Haydn and Mozart, performing before an invited audience; a generation later, the darling of the palace circuit was the wild-eyed Ludwig van Beethoven.

One of Vienna's modern wonders is the way most of these ancient theaters have been preserved. One can still take in intimate opera at the theater out at Schönbrunn Palace, sung on a stage Mozart once trod; the Theater an der Wien, where Beethoven's *Fidelio* was first heard, still houses opera. The palaces are still there, too, but most of them are now embassies or corporate headquarters—with the ghostly sounds of Haydn's violin and Mozart's viola mingling with the Muzak.

He was, by mid-1788, deeply in debt—to a former landlord, to a pawnbroker, and to his friend and fellow Freemason, Michael Puchberg, to whom he wrote letter after letter, each more pitiful, begging for monetary loans. "Great God!" he wrote in one note, "I would not wish my worst enemy to be in my present situation. And if you, most beloved friend and brother, forsake me, we are altogether lost...". Four out of the six Mozart children had died, at birth or soon after. The family continually moved into less expensive quarters, in Vienna or out in the suburbs. Leopold Mozart had died in 1787, still partially estranged from his son; a conciliatory letter from Wolfgang, written after Leopold's death, may have cleansed his conscience but hardly sufficed to bridge the gap. To make matters worse, Mozart himself became progressively ill, probably from a kidney ailment. Between him and Constanze, there was hardly a day since their marriage when they both had the good health to truly enjoy each other's company.

Yet this misery may have been somewhat exaggerated by the more romantic biographers. By 1790, Mozart had gained a somewhat firmer control over his finances and had even begun to repay his debts. In his last years, too, he had begun an investigation into the music of Johann Sebastian Bach, most of which still lay uncatalogued and unpublished. A Viennese dilettante, Baron Gottfried van Swieten, had made his own studies of Bach's music and had amassed a collection of manuscripts which he invited Mozart to peruse. His discoveries, especially of the richness of Bach's mastery of **counterpoint,** had a profound effect on Mozart's own musical outlook. In the amazing finale to the *Jupiter*, the last of the symphonies, the spirit of Bach looks on approvingly as five separate themes are combined in smooth and effortless counterpoint—a dazzling effect.

Così fan tutte, the third collaboration with Da Ponte, had had only a middling success at its Vienna premiere in early 1790; a cynical comedy about human weakness on the battlefield of love, the work's delicious subtlety has only been recognized in the twentieth century.

One more joyous comedy remained in Mozart's pen, this time in German and

The Magic Flute *title page: Papageno the bird-catcher was the most popular character in Mozart's opera.*

reverting to the lightweight form that had reaped success for the *Seraglio* nine years earlier: *The Magic Flute*. The plot is not easily explained, especially since the good guys become the bad guys halfway through the first act. Still, it is possible to make out the magnificent underlying themes: sacred and profane love, high moral principles, and the need for humans to laugh at themselves now and then. Emanuel Schikaneder was the librettist; the work was written for Schikaneder's popular folk theater, with a potpourri of musical styles—from happy buffoonery to music that, according to playwright

A recreation by W. Shields of the famous scene: Mozart on the last night of his life, singing through the Requiem *with several of his friends attendant at his bedside.*

George Bernard Shaw, "could be put into the mouth of God without blasphemy"—that could almost serve as a summary of Mozart's broad musical outlook.

Soon the awareness of death's presence took hold. In July 1791, a mysterious stranger appeared at Mozart's door, bearing an offer to compose a *Requiem* as a well-paid commission. Mozart was in no position to refuse, but he was also hardly in a position to bring the work to completion. His letters suggest that fear was guiding his pen; it was also clear, in the strength and breadth of the choral writing, that Mozart had made an ultimate reconciliation with his studies of Bach.

But he did not live to finish the work. On the night of 4 December 1791, Constanze, Mozart's pupil Franz Süssmayr, and several others gathered around the composer's sickbed and sang through the completed sections of the *Requiem*. A doctor applied cold poultices to Mozart's head to alleviate the fever, but this treatment induced a coma instead. Shortly after midnight, six weeks before his thirty-sixth birthday, Mozart died. The funeral service, contrary to many myths, was well-attended. In accordance with a decree of Emperor Joseph, passed for sanitary reasons, Mozart's body was carried beyond the city walls and interred in a common grave—not the pauper's burial of legend, but not an elegant end, either.

A memorial in Prague, ten days later, brought out thousands who, according to newspaper accounts, "shed countless tears." A few weeks after that, there was a proper service in Vienna, as well. Antonio Salieri conducted. The rumor that he had poisoned his presumed rival grew out of delusions that assailed Salieri himself in his own last days; the story was perpetuated in a short play by Aleksandr Pushkin, *Mozart and Salieri*, that Nikolai Rimski-Korsakoff turned into a rather charming opera, and in the extravagant falsification in Peter Shaffer's *Amadeus*. Actually, Salieri went on to a distinguished career as a pedagogue. His pupils included Ludwig van Beethoven and Franz Schubert; there is no record that he regarded either of them as rivals.

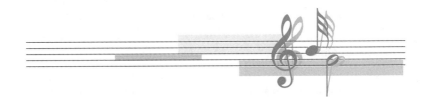

Mozart After Mozart

o

NEITHER POVERTY NOR NEGLECT killed Mozart. Practitioners of a particular form of forensic medicine that seeks to establish the cause of death of famous figures of the past have pinpointed his ultimate ailment as a form of rheumatic fever, an affliction that continued to claim worthy lives until the invention of modern antibiotics. His doctors probably contributed to his early death by continually prescribing bleeding, a common but frequently lethal practice of the time. Constanze was not too competent in dealing with her late husband's affairs—but not too incompetent, either. Historians seem to take particular delight in portraying her less favorable side, as a sex kitten, a scatterbrain, a spendthrift without whose extravagances Mozart might have lived a full and healthy existence.

True, Constanze seems to have gone to pieces at her husband's bedside; one authenticated story has her crawling into the bed to try to catch Wolfgang's illness (it was probably not contagious). Yet it was she who arranged for Mozart's pupil Franz Xavier Süssmayr to finish the *Requiem*, for which Mozart had completed more than half the work and left sketches for a good deal more. Perhaps relatedly, there is also some evidence that Constanze and Süssmayr were more than just good friends.

In the years immediately following Mozart's death, Constanze waged a frustrating war to get some kind of pension from the government and finally had to settle for a degrading pittance. Still, she worked hard on Wolfgang's behalf, arranging benefit concerts and putting his manuscripts in some kind of order. Largely through her efforts, the press and, thus, the world were finally made aware of the qualities of her late husband's music, as they had not been during his lifetime. In one of the concerts she arranged, during Lent of 1795, the *Piano Concerto No. 20* was performed between the two acts of the opera *La clemenza di Tito*. The pianist for the event was twenty-four-year-old Ludwig van Beethoven, recently arrived in Vienna from his native Bonn, and already making a name in Vienna as a piano virtuoso. Obviously stirred by the music—which he

A formal portrait of the composer.

invoked more than once in his own works—Beethoven later wrote down the cadenzas he improvised in that performance, which some brave pianists still attempt today.

Mindful of Wolfgang's triumphs as a child prodigy, Constanze was determined to engineer a similar career for the youngest of their six children, Franz Xaver, born only five months before his father's death. In Prague, on 17 November 1797, she produced another of those tremendous concerts that included concertos, symphonies, arias, operatic ensembles, and a chorus celebrating the outbreak of peace in the Napoleonic Wars (the treaty of Campo

Beethoven (1770-1827): He visited Mozart on his first trip to Vienna, and Mozart is reported to have been impressed. Later Beethoven was soloist in Mozart's D-minor Piano Concerto, and composed cadenzas which have survived.

Formio was made the previous month)—all with music by the late Mozart. An entry on the program begged "forbearance at this first attempt to display the gentle talents" of the six-year-old Franz Xaver Wolfgang Mozart, who would "attempt to follow the great example of his father" by singing an aria from *The Magic Flute*. Franz Xaver (1791-1844) did have a modest career as a musician and composer, but his music is listened to today primarily for its curiosity value.

Constanze, then, continued to live relatively comfortably on

Wolfgang's music. She remarried, and her second husband's tomb-stone identifies him merely as "Mozart's widow's second spouse."

Throughout the nineteenth century, Mozart's legacy was variously regarded. The romantics adored the demoniac in his works, not only *Don Giovanni* but also the *Piano Concerto in D Minor* and the *Symphony No. 40*—anything, in fact, in a minor key. Adoration did not always equal understanding, however. In keeping with the classical ideal of balance, Mozart and Da Ponte had concluded their *Don Giovanni*, after the Don has been dragged down to his just D-minor reward among the fires of Hades, with a sextet in which the couples the villain had victimized look forward to a happier future and hand down a D-major moralistic message to the audience ("Behave yourselves, or share his fate"). The romantics preferred the D-minor conclusion, and so for almost a century the rightful ending—which to the eighteenth-century sensibility restored the balance and brought the drama full circle—languished unheard, until Gustav Mahler reinstituted it during his time as head of the Vienna State Opera. The tidier, more classical side of Mozart—the exquisite balance in, say, the *Piano Concerto No. 21*—interested the romantics less.

There were exceptions among romantic writers, of course, along with some curious ideas. To Robert Schumann, influential both as composer and critic, Mozart's *Symphony No. 40* was "a work in which every note is golden, every movement a treasure." That said, Schumann goes on to question the sanity of a passage in the slow

movement, in which Mozart twists the harmony around in a remarkably prophetic manner. "These measures simply do not belong," sniffs
Schumann—as if to say "How dare this upstart Mozart anticipate
some of my own harmonic turns almost half a century ago?"—and
he recommends their being cut from performances. Contradictory
as it might seem, Richard Wagner adored Mozart's music. So did
Pyotr Ilich Tchaikovsky, who went so far as to recast some of Mozart's
piano works as an orchestral suite entitled *Mozartiana*.

By the twentieth century, a worldwide understanding of Mozart
was an uneven affair. Richard Strauss firmly believed that in at least

Reality Bites

The eighteenth-century artist had
fewer qualms than today's creator,
especially on matters of plagiarism
and downright fakery. It is known,
for example, that the mysterious
stranger who came to Mozart to
commission the *Requiem* was actually an emissary from a certain
Viennese dilettante, Count Franz
von Walsegg, who wanted this
particular work as a memorial to
his late wife and whose peculiar
pleasure was to bestow generous
commissions on struggling com-

posers and pass the works off as
his own. Purity in such affairs was
not yet in the air; Mozart himself
composed a number of arias to be
inserted in the operas of others—
with, or just as often without,
credit.

As Mozart's fame spread after his
death, dozens of works by other,
lesser composers appeared on the
market with Mozart's name at-
tached. There is, for example, a
pompous piece of choral writing
that was once greatly prized by
British choral groups, called the
Gloria from the Twelfth Mass; a

two of his operas, *Der Rosenkavalier* and *Ariadne auf Naxos*, he had found the way to re-express the Mozartian spirit in contemporary trappings. Sergei Prokofiev accomplished this even more successfully, within smaller dimensions, in his *Classical Symphony*; Igor Stravinsky's clear, meticulous, dry-point works of the years following the cataclysms of *The Rite of Spring* do seem to restore an eighteenth-century balance, though without the warmth of their inspired prototype.

Meanwhile, Mozart's music itself limped along. Old recordings, many of them reissued on CD, attest to the distortions that

tinkly composition called *Pastorale variée* is still inflicted upon unknowing piano students; and the Schirmer edition of piano sonatas used to conclude with a hideous and clearly spurious piece in B-flat, which got tangled up in the "wrong" keys in the finale and extricated itself only with the clumsiest heave-ho.

Better than any of these is a work by Mozart himself that purposely attempts to plagiarize the humble efforts of nugatory composers of the era. The *Musical Joke* (K. 522) mercilessly parodies these poor dodos' efforts to move to a contrasting key-area via a theme that keeps falling back on itself, guffaws as the first violinist attempts a cadenza with no idea of what to do next, and roars with laughter as a pair of horn players totally mess up what is clearly intended as a passionate tune. Mozart himself must have been shocked at the raucous bad manners of his piece; days later, he created the sublime *Eine kleine Nachtmusik* (K. 525), which set matters straight.

were visited upon the music: coloratura sopranos adding their own anachronistic frostings to their big aria in *The Magic Flute;* even the great Toscanini torturing the lines in the *Haffner* symphony way out of shape. Yet there were great and honest Mozart performances even back then: the wonderful Irish tenor John McCormack breaking hearts in 1915 with an aria from *Don Giovanni,* or Richard Strauss extracting the full drama from the *Symphony No. 40* in an ancient recording from 1928. *Don Giovanni,* with or without its final resolution, has held the stage continuously, and somewhere or other someone is always staging *The Magic Flute.* But that most human of

Mozart monument: One of many Mozart memorials throughout Austria, this one stands in Salzburg, not far from his birthplace.

comedies, *The Marriage of Figaro,* went twenty-three years without a performance at the Metropolitan Opera until it was revived in the 1940s; *Così fan tutte* only received its first American staging in 1922, a full 133 years after its creation.

The estimation of Mozart's music slumped back to the delicate Dresden-china-and-crystal image in some circles in the first decades of the 1900s, however. Only with the advocacy of conductor Sir Thomas Beecham (who made the first recordings of the symphonies that resembled the proportions of Mozart's orchestras), the pianist

Artur Schnabel (who played and recorded the concertos with an awareness of their melodic and harmonic depths), and Fritz Busch (who conducted and recorded the operas in the properly intimate setting of Britain's Glyndebourne) was there something like a restoration of Mozart's proper place in the musical world. By 1941, the 150th anniversary year of Mozart's death, small orchestras around the world began once again to play his music correctly.

What does "correct" mean in this instance? In Mozart's time, nobody bothered much about the proper performance of bygone music; aside from church music, in fact, almost everything brought to the concert stage in the 1780s was new, or at least the work of living composers. There were no scholarly editions of the music from the past, no pianists or conductors arguing that what little bygone music there was—a Bach or Vivaldi concerto, perhaps, or a Handel concerto grosso—needed to be restored to "the way the composer heard it," as the current directive goes.

Now, of course, there is an obsession with correcting the so-called errors of contemporary performers of early music. It is important, or so it is said, to perform Mozart concertos on a "Mozart" piano, softer in tone than the concert grand and more limited in range, perhaps, but better at blending in with orchestral instruments. These instruments, too, must be of eighteenth-century design: with strings of sheep gut instead of steel, bows less tautly wound than those of today, the horns and trumpets without valves, the wood-

The Changing Image

In October 1993, scientists at a California neurobiology institute confirmed what many people already knew: that listening to Mozart was good for the brain. College students exposed to ten minutes of the *Sonata for Two Pianos* (K. 448) experienced an immediate rise in their I.Q. scores. (One might ask what would happen if the students had been allowed to listen to the entire twenty-four minutes of the *Sonata,* but these are fast-moving times.) It's easy enough to fathom the ingredients in this Mozartian prescription: the exact blend of wit, grace, structural integrity, and off-center surprises that sweeps the listener into the music's headlong progression. Needless to say, this sonata is not the only work of Mozart's the researchers might have used.

This view of Mozart—as the amalgam of original beauty and structural rationale—did not always prevail. His operas were simultane-ously adored and mutilated; *Così fan tutte,* when performed at all in the nineteenth century, was decked out with a new story line and libretto; *Don Giovanni* was deemed better-suited to the Romantic image if the final sextet were omitted. Norwegian composer Edvard Grieg wrote a long article defending Mozart from the "musicians of our time who are so far advanced that they care no longer to hear Mozart's music"—but Grieg himself devised second-piano accompaniments "to impart to several of Mozart's pianoforte sonatas a tonal effect appealing to our modern ears."

Not many recordings of Mozart's music were undertaken in the pre-electric days; those that were—the *Figaro* overture on a 1914 disc by the legendary Arthur Nikisch, some arias from *Figaro* and *The Magic Flute,* a couple of short piano pieces—are so distorted with tempo changes, unstylish interpolations, and the like as to suggest that the image of Mozart as brain food was very far down the road.

Yet there are hugely dramatic, explosive early electrical recordings by the Netherlands' Willem Mengelberg and the redoubtable Richard Strauss that suggest the initial stages in the campaign to restore Mozart's reputation as a dramatic genius. The earliest recording of a complete piano concerto, *No. 17* (K. 453), made in Budapest in 1928 with Ernst von Dohnanyi conducting from the keyboard (still available on the Koch-Schwann label) is a fascinating version: a highly romanticized approach, the tempos sometimes excruciatingly slow, with a great deal of strength. Along with Arturo Toscanini's 1929 *Haffner* Symphony with the New York Philharmonic, it is the best example of the old-fashioned, "personalized" Mozart that contemporary taste seems to deplore. (Toscanini's 1946 *Haffner* with the NBC Symphony is far more "straight" and far less interesting. Both performances are in RCA's complete Toscanini series.)

Among pianists, the ideal of Mozart's music as the personification of tinkling chandeliers and Dresden figurines was harder to dispel. It persisted in the performances of the French pianist Robert Casadesus, who recorded both sonatas and concertos for Columbia, and in a 1932 recording by Artur (as he spelled it then) Rubinstein of the *Concerto No. 23* (K. 488). But Mozart remained a closed door to Rubinstein, as well as to his formidable contemporary Vladimir Horowitz. Of their generation, the Austrians Artur Schnabel and Rudolf Serkin sensed the undertones and overtones in Mozart's music; Serkin, furthermore, communicated them to later generations through his teaching and his presence at the Marlboro Festival in Vermont, whence today's "intellectual" Mozart gang—Serkin's son Peter, Murray Perahia, Emanuel Ax, etc.—drew its sustenance. Alfred Brendel, Vienna-born, and Mitsuko Uchida, Vienna-trained, round out the roster of musicians whose approach to Mozart embodies the findings of those Californian I.Q. testers—and proves them gloriously correct.

This highly idealized portrait is an engraving by Paul Burfus after the painting by Franz Schwüer.

winds similarly primitive. Soloists are expected to observe the rules of ornamentation, trills, and other "doodles" applied to the notes of a melody to make it sound different each time around. Leopold Mozart's treatise on violin playing is a valuable source of information on the subject of ornamentation. Alfred Brendel uses a discreet amount of ornamentation in the slow movements of both Mozart concertos on this recording. And, while no exact guideposts exist to indicate the proper tempos in Mozart's day— what he meant by "allegro," for example— enough secondary evidence exists to convince many authenticity advocates that music tended to chug along at a faster clip than most traditionalist conductors choose nowadays. (The difference in resonance between a Mozart-era hall, capacity 200, and a 3,000-seat modern concert hall must also influence matters of tempo.)

The crux of this "authenticity" business is, of course, the ears and expectations of the audience. The audience of 1785 could be stirred, even shocked, by the dramatic onslaught at the start of the *Piano Concerto in D Minor*, shocked again at the sudden outburst midway in the slow movement, and surprised and delighted at the rollicking D-major ending of the last movement after all the D-minor devilry. Today, these high effects sound quaint and charming; after all, modern audiences have been through the battles of the monsters in Wagner's *Ring of the Nibelung* or Stravinsky's *The Rite of Spring*. They have heard the Rolling Stones and Tibetan chants. The listener can still be rendered molten by the slow movement of the *Piano Concerto in C Major*, but the music is heard within a 200-year-old frame of reference, and it can not be otherwise.

Strict authenticity—the scrupulous restoration of the sounds Mozart or Haydn might have heard at a performance—is for today's audiences pretty much self-defeating. A careful, "authentic" Mozart performance, employing something close to his instruments and in the proportions of his own orchestra, can, of course, be a lovely thing, given dedicated musicians who are responsive to what lies in the music itself. Another kind of meticulous Mozart performance, using modern instruments played with taste and regard for the proportions in the music, can be equally moving. No better proof exists of the universality of his music.

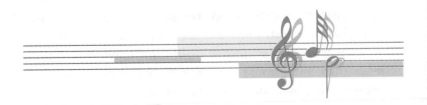

Play by Play:
Mozart's Reinvention of the Piano Concerto

BY 1785, MOZART WAS REASONABLY well-off in Vienna—as comfortable as he would ever be. His opera the *Abduction from the Seraglio*, which had served as his musical entrée into Viennese cultural circles, was still happily remembered three years after its premiere. At the court of the Emperor Joseph II, a moderately perceptive connoisseur by all accounts, Mozart was prized both as a composer and a piano virtuoso. Audiences flocked to his frequent public concerts, which included a phenomenally popular series given during the Lenten season, when the opera houses were closed and instrumental music reigned unchallenged. This series of concertos (seventeen in all) came to represent—even more than his splendid run of forty-plus symphonies—the expressive height of Mozart's instrumental legacy.

Two kinds of musical thought come together in these extraordinary works, the symphonic and the vocal. The generic structural features of the instrumental concerto had taken shape in the preceding decades, in the works of Sebastian Bach's two most illustrious sons, Carl Philipp Emanuel and Johann Christian, and a few of their ordinarily capable imitators. The typical form consisted of three movements, with the first being the most extended and complex, the last, the most brilliant and crowd-pleasing, with a quiet, expressive, slow movement in between.

The first movement was built along the typical sonata-form pattern, with melodic material in contrasting keys, gradually developed in a greater variety of keys, and then returning all in the same key. Two further features peculiar to the concerto enhanced the form. The movement began with a purely orchestral presentation of some, perhaps all, of the movement's material, all in the same key and designed to build anticipation for the soloist's eventual appearance. There then ensued the "normal" first-movement form, for soloist and orchestra, presenting the material of the movement and moving from the original key to new keys and then back again. But then, at the end of the first movement, before a final rounding-off, all orchestral activity stopped while the soloist improvised a **cadenza**, usually based on the themes of the movement (but sometimes based on whatever the soloist happened to have in mind). There might also be other cadenzas along the way, whenever the music passed through an important structural juncture. All of this new concerto-oriented garnishment related, of course, to the virtuosic demands of the form, the need to create a dramatic entrance for the soloist at the start, and a dramatic solo turn near the end.

The slow movement and finale were usually simpler in structure. The former might consist of a long, flowing melody for soloist, accompanied very discreetly by the orchestra, with perhaps a contrasting middle section and then a return, with or without the possibility of another solo cadenza. The last movement might return to the same kind of sonata-form complexity as the first, it might be a set of variations (with an increasingly difficult solo part to placate the soloist and the fans out front), or the A-B-A-C-A-D-A... -form of the rondo.

The young Mozart had observed these rubrics quite literally in his boyhood concertos. What distinguishes his later forays into the concerto form was his growing mastery of vocal music, especially of opera. Listen, for example, to the most famous moment from his teen-age operas, the aria "L'amerò, sarò constante" from *Il ré pastore:* it's really a concerto for two soloists, the singer and a violin. So alike in spirit are these two parts that they could be interchanged without losing the sweet, ecstatic effect.

And so the concerto ideal—the piano concerto most of all, but also the concertos for violin, horn, clarinet, and the miraculous *Sinfonia Concertante for Violin and Viola*—became, for Mozart, a kind of wordless opera. The melodies were conceived as dialogues: a questioning phrase, an answering phrase. For one of a thousand examples, listen to the very opening of the *Piano Concerto in C Major:* a quiet figure that one critic describes as "a march on tiptoes," with a more flowing answering figure from the high strings, and a joyous closing theme from the full orchestra, including martial trumpets and drums. Listen then to the serene, haunting piano melody in the slow movement, that seems to go on and on without pausing for breath, but also indulges in wide skips all over the quiet, throbbing accompaniment; it could be an aria for some warmhearted but troubled character in a Mozart opera—the Countess in *The Marriage of Figaro*, perhaps. Another example is the joyous D-major resolution that dispels the D-minor furor at the end of the *D-minor Concerto;* it's like the finale of *Figaro*, with everybody eager to share in the joy after the dark night of trickery and deception.

Even before the products of his Vienna years, Mozart's concertos are full of experiments that try to get around the strictness of the "rules" while still respecting the classical spirit. In the *Piano Concerto in E-flat* (K. 271) from 1777, Mozart allows his soloist to break in at the start of what is supposed to be—and always had been—the purely orchestral introduction. In that concerto, too, the momentum of the bubbling finale is interrupted by a surprising and unexpected twist: a slow minuet. And it is in that concerto, as well, that Mozart's power to touch the heart with slow, melancholy, floating melodies for the solo pianist, over the simplest orchestral accompaniment, comes into full realization.

The seventeen Vienna concertos, however, represent the culmination of Mozart's expressive instrumental writing—the culmination as well, one might say, of the dramatic possibilities of the classical style. The young Ludwig van Beethoven, whose one-time hopes of studying with Mozart were thwarted by his idol's early death, is known to have expressed both envy and frustration after hearing one of these concertos. The magnificence of Beethoven's own concertos came about through his continuation of Mozart's loosening of the strict ties of classical form; in fact, it is fair to suggest Mozart as one of the great enabling forces for Beethoven's onslaughts on the "normal" musical practices of his time.

Every one of the Vienna concertos is a world unto itself; no two are alike at any point. The two concertos on this CD bring home that point; composed within weeks of one another (in the early months of 1785), they seemingly breathe the air of different planets. The *D-minor Concerto* seethes with fury; its opening theme murmurs behind a dark mask, its rhythms elusive, its melodic outline clouded over.

Did Beethoven invoke this mysterious, muttering beginning when he shaped the similar opening of his *Ninth Symphony*—also in D minor, and also emerging from what sounds like outer space? He knew the *Concerto* and even composed a proud, passionate cadenza for it that some pianists occasionally attempt.

The *C-major Concerto* couldn't be further removed from the *D-minor:* its opening is clean and distinct, punctuated with what sound like fanfares from toy trumpets and drums; its famous slow movement, a single breath of melody like a star's track across a midnight sky. In the late twentieth century, that movement has led a life of its own—in the bittersweet, visually gorgeous Swedish film *Elvira Madigan,* it serves as the principal music, agonizingly faded down time and again just as the audience becomes hypnotized by its flow. At least it got Mozart onto the charts; he hadn't always been that fortunate.

A note on these analyses: Elsewhere in this volume is an explanation of the ideals of classicism as they relate to an obsession with structural neatness, logic, and symmetry. This provides a glimpse of the intricate craft of composition as it flourished late in the eighteenth century, of how composers were meticulous in their manipulation of music in various keys (including the systematic manner of departure from the main key of a work into contrasting key-areas and the eventual return), of how the order of themes at the start of a movement is mirrored when they all return later on. Also included are facts about the special structure of the first movement of classical concertos—how, for example, the orchestral introduction (**ritornello**) presents the material of the movement, all in the tonic key, which the soloist-plus-orchestra then expands upon in several keys.

Be prepared, however, for the sublime stretching of these rules in every one of Mozart's mature instrumental works, his constant testing of the limits of classical structure. Just the first few minutes of the *D-minor Concerto* present a veritable police blotter of violations: the mysterious, cloud-wrapped opening theme, the change of key within the ritornello, the piano's entrance with a theme not previously hinted at. By the end of this movement, however, the logic of Mozart's design has brought everything into its proper place; expression and structure have achieved their equilibrium.

One way to follow the quirks of Mozart's design, and his ingenuity in manipulating the interplay of structural unity and contrast, is to assign letters to all the melodic elements in each movement: A, B, C, etc. Each element should be easily identifiable by matching it against the elapsed-time indication.

Piano Concerto No. 20 in D Minor (K. 466)

Scoring: *piano, flute, two oboes, two bassoons, two horns, two trumpets, timpani, and strings. Completed 10 February 1785.*

First movement: *Allegro*

Rather than the customary clear-cut classical theme, Mozart concocts a beginning **[T1/i1, 0:00]**, out of swirling mists, a melody on the rhythmic off-beats (A) and a muttering, drumlike figure in the lower strings (B). Out of the murk eventually emerges **[T1/i1, 0:26]** a sweeping, demonic, defiant theme in D minor (C) that achieves a furious cadence [T1/i1, 0:47]. A contrasting, quiet theme (D), a dialogue within the wind section in F major [T1/i1, 0:56], lets the listener catch a moment's breath, but the D-minor fury returns with a new tapestry of themes: a stormy figure (E) [T1/i1, 1:17] that rushes all over the place, and then a quiet rounding-off melody (F) [T1/i1, 2:00] that throttles the music down to near silence.

The soloist first appears [T1/i2, 2:12] with a melancholy theme (G) the listener hasn't heard before, but will hear again soon. This leads to the complex of ideas (A, B, C) [T1/i2, 2:41] that began the movement, but this time involving both the pianist and the orchestra. The "conversational" theme (D) now becomes a conversation between the piano and the orchestral winds [T1/i2, 3:21], coming to an anticipatory cadence.

A new theme (H) [T1/i3, 3:44] provides contrast; its F-major sweetness and jauntiness is like a comforting hand. Stated first by the piano, with flickers of light from the strings, the theme is repeated [T1/i3, 4:12] by the piano and winds. In all his late piano concertos, this chamber-musiclike texture of piano versus winds seems to be Mozart's favorite sound. His *Quintet for Piano and Winds* (K. 452) dates from the same period as this concerto, and Mozart described it as "his best composition so far." But that was before *Figaro, Don Giovanni*, or, indeed, this concerto.

Here, the stormy theme (E) from the end of the orchestral ritornello returns [T1/i3, 4:29], somewhat tamer in mood. It has moved, after all, into the relatively sunnier precincts of F major.

The orchestra bursts in to start the development **[T1/i4, 5:04]**, with reminiscences of themes (B, C, and F) still anchored in F major but starting to show signs of restlessness. The piano "remembers" its distinctive entrance theme (G) **[T1/i4, 5:37],** and this develops into an eloquent argument between that theme in the piano and the mysterious orchestral mutterings (A, B) **[T1/i4, 6:01]** that began the work. The piano keeps trying to expand its theme; the orchestral grumblings recur to cap the lid on the soloist's rhapsodizing. Meanwhile, the music moves constantly through a sequence of keys, adding to the sense of rootlessness. Finally **[T1/i4, 7:04]**, at the height of harmonic incertitude, piano and orchestra join forces and find their way back. Under sustained wind chords, the piano engages in a long, spaced-out rumination, while the drumlike figure (B) from the opening sounds in the bass, becoming ever more persistent, driving the music forward to some goal. The last few bars of this sequence belong to the piano alone, muttering in its low register and moving in one stark gesture back to the initial key of D minor to start the recapitulation.

The music returns **[T1/i5, 7:25]** to that mysterious, buzzing, fragmentary beginning (A, B, C)—now, however, involving both piano and orchestra. Again, the stormy D-minor theme (D) from the ritornello, which Mozart had bypassed in the full exposition, now returns **[T1/i5, 7:50]**, also as a dialogue between piano and orchestra. According to the practice of the time, the material from the exposition can be expected to return now in the recapitulation, but all in the same key. That, indeed, is the case with the reappearance of the "conversational" theme (D) and the jaunty F-major theme (H). Their return **[T1/i6, 8:23, 8:49]** does, in fact, follow "normal" practice, with the key-change (F major to D minor) greatly affecting the expressive nature of the music. The piano erupts once again **[T1/i6, 9:38]** with the first of the two themes (E) that had closed out the ritornello; the orchestra restates the great stormy theme (D) **[T1/i6, 10:22]** from the ritornello, then breaks off **[T1/i7, 10:40]**.

No cadenza in Mozart's hand survives, although there is an interesting one by Beethoven that some pianists favor. Alfred Brendel's own cadenza reflects his awareness of the uniqueness of this concerto, as a bridge to a much later mode of expression. The cadenza is short, but it ends with a rush, with the orchestra **[T1/i8, 12:27]** presenting the two closing themes (E,F) from the ritornello and then subsiding to a near-silence. The final music in this extraordinary movement is brand-new, a return of the drumlike theme (B) **[T1/i8, 13:10]** as accompaniment to a whole new melody as the music retreats back toward the shadows from which it had come.

Just to demonstrate the flexibility in Mozart's handling of the presentation-plus-repeat aspects of the classical concerto form, here is a brief overview of this first movement:

Ritornello	Exposition	Development	Recapitulation	Cadenza	Coda
ABCD-EF	G-ABCD-H-E	BCF-G+AB-B	ABC-D-H-E-D	B+H	EF+B

Second movement: *Romanze*

Mozart specified no tempo marking (e.g., andante, adagio*) for this movement, although the notation "Romanze" leaves little doubt.*

The opening is a spacious, elegant paragraph consisting of two matched sections (A, B), each with its theme stated first by the piano alone [T2/i1, 0:00, 0:48] and answered by the orchestra [T2/i1, 0:14, 1:00]. Each "answer" begins on an upbeat, which the ear assumes would be played by the ensuing performing force. Charmingly, Mozart foils this expectation each time; the piano plays the three-note upbeat to the orchestral answer and vice versa. It's a small detail, but one of the million similar effects that account for Mozart's unique flow. The second orchestral answer extends [T2/i1, 1:23] to provide a ravishing closing theme (C) [T2/i1, 1:47].

An even more ravishing theme (D) now ensues [T2/i2, 1:58], little more than a one-finger solo for the pianist over a steadily pulsating accompaniment. The key (B-flat major) remains the same, and so does the mood. It might be an operatic aria, for a character of exuberant but tender heart (Cherubino in *Figaro*, perhaps); as a piano solo, it brings that unwieldy instrument as close to human speech as any composer would ever attain—at least until Mozart's next concerto, that is. When people compile their lists of the most sublime Mozartian moments, this brief episode is almost always included. A touch of minor harmony darkens the tune's second strain [T2/i2,

2:35] but is soon dispelled in an almost giddy final phrase [T2/i2, 2:59], which blends into a reprise of theme (C) and leads to what starts as a return of theme (A) [T2/i2, 3:27], the piano solo followed by orchestra, as before. This only gets as far as the first section, however, when...

BANG! The scene is suddenly transformed; the serene B-flat landscape becomes a flame-strewn, rocky path in G minor (Mozart's most-used key for a frigid, tragic utterance—compare the *Symphony No. 40* and the *G-minor String Quintet*). The tempo doesn't change, but the sense of momentum does; the speedup is simply the result of more things happening on each beat in each measure. The piano sweeps up and down [T2/i3, 4:16, repeat 4:37], the tune (E) in the upper range echoed in the lower, the orchestral winds doubling the piano and supplying a further counterpoint. Each half of this two-part outburst is repeated. In the second half [T2/i3, 4:58, repeat 5:40] the echoing between piano and winds takes place at shorter intervals, further tightening the emotional screws.

The momentum gradually slackens [T2/i3, 6:30] and the tune (E) seems to disintegrate. Listen for Mozart's subtle, supple way of slowing the music, like a race-car driver downshifting. The notes themselves gradually lengthen. The sixteenth-note triplets become normal sixteenth notes, then eighth-note triplets, which become normal eighth notes, at which time [T2/i4, 6:50] the motion has been sufficiently braked to allow for a reprise of theme (A). Only the piano has the first part of the theme this time; only the orchestra has the second (as opposed to the piano/orchestra alternation in both sections earlier), and the dramatic closing theme (C) begins in the orchestra with gentle, rippling runs and **arpeggios** from the piano.

"Begins," that is. The ear may sense that the end of this movement is approaching, but Mozart's fund of ideas hasn't run out. Theme (C) breaks off after the first of its two phrases; the winds interrupt with a further, gentle closing idea that hasn't been heard before (F) [T2/i5, 8:16]; this is taken up by the piano. Only then does the delicate closing phrase of theme (C) bring the movement to a close [T2/i5, 8:54]. Even at this point, however, there is one more elegant detail in the music's very last breath; listen carefully, as the piano plays its last B-flat arpeggio not on the beat, as expected, but between the beats—a reminiscence, perhaps, of the off-the-beat figures that began this concerto way back in Track 1. Either way, it's another one of those details that help establish Mozart's uniqueness.

Third movement: *Rondo, allegro assai* (*assai* = "**rather**")

Scholars have a name for the kind of theme that begins this exuberant, fiery movement: it's called a "Mannheim Rocket." Composers at the court at Mannheim (e.g., Johann Stamitz, Ignaz Holzbauer) were fond of a particular kind of theme that began low and zoomed upward. (Another example: the opening of Beethoven's Piano Sonata, Op. 2, No. 1.)

The piano starts theme (A) alone **[T3/i1, 0:00]**, with a series of leaps and plunges that nearly reaches the upper limit of the instrument in Mozart's time. The orchestra picks up the theme **[T3/i1, 0:12]** and immediately pushes forward into new harmonic regions; the speed at which things happen here contrasts with the relaxation at the end of the second movement. A fierce closing idea (B) **[T3/i1, 0:26]** is hurled out by winds and strings, against a throbbing repeated-note accompaniment in the lower strings, to round out this first section. The piano re-enters with what sounds like a whole new approach (C) **[T3/i2, 0:54]**, but it soon merges back into theme (A) **[T3/i2, 1:03]**. A long transition passage, a teeming complex of new thematic thoughts and fragments, hurtles onward; one theme (D) for piano alone **[T3/i3, 1:19]**, and another (E) for piano and strings, consisting of a series of descending-note passages **[T3/i3, 1:36]**, leads finally to a point of rest. It's amazing, the number of different notions Mozart has crammed into these two minutes; it's also amazing, in the course of the movement, how skillfully he devises new and separate uses for each of them.

Now, in a tranquil change to F major, a new, lyrical theme (F) **[T3/i4, 1:59]** is first presented by the strings, immediately thereafter by the piano; it sails along blithely but then **[T3/i4, 2:24]** takes on a scowl as minor-key harmonies move in like clouds across a bright sky. The music comes to a half-cadence full of anticipation.

Theme (A) returns in the piano, in D minor as before **[T3/i5,**

2:41], but the orchestral extension [T3/i5, 2:52] moves off into new key-areas. This is a structural hybrid: a combination of rondo form—the return of (A) after ensuing material—and the features of a sonata-form development section, with the rapidly changing keys and a fragmentation of some of the previously-heard thematic material. In what must be regarded as a nominational cop-out, this hybrid form bears a hybrid name: rondo-sonata.

Following the orchestral extension, the piano returns with theme (C) [T3/i5, 3:05], which breaks off for a return of fragments from theme (A). A conversation ensues between piano and winds, centering around these fragments [T3/i5, 3:19]. Then, the conversation turns to an examination of theme (C) [T3/i5, 3:34], and this moves on, often somewhat skittishly. At this point, the matter of theme (D) is taken up; by now, the music has settled back in the home key of D minor, sliding into a return of harmonic stability after the many vagaries of the previous few moments.

One of two things may have happened. Either the recapitulation began with the return of theme (A) in D minor at [2:41], which was then interrupted by the long development, or the recapitulation has now begun, and the return of theme (A) has been bypassed. In any case, the composer has magically brought the music back to the stability of home base, after some interesting travels.

Theme (F)—the comforting, lyrical theme in F major that was first heard at [1:59]—now returns in D minor [T3/i6, 4:36], bearing a whole new set of emotional colors from the key-change, and leading to a stormy outbreak **[T3/i6, 5:08]**, still in D minor; this torrent recalls the violent closing theme (B) at the start of the movement. At this point, another brief cadenza is in order. Instead of the customary brief ending following the cadenza, Mozart turns on a whole new set of lights to end this volatile movement. The key is now D major; theme (F) casts off its melancholy garb from its previous appearance and now shines forth resplendent **[T3/i7, 6:08]**, outfitted with a new subsequent phrase **[T3/i7, 6:28]** for full orchestra and piano. There's more: theme (F) takes on a whole new twist **[T3/i7, 6:40]** that includes a delicious closing flourish from horn and trumpet, repeated and echoed by the other winds. With a final scurry by the piano, followed by the full orchestra, the concerto ends on a note of delight— a surprising but fulfilling benevolent note after the storms that have gone before.

Piano Concerto No. 21 in C (K. 467)

Scoring: *Piano, flute, two oboes, two bassoons, two horns, two trumpets, timpani, and strings. Completed 9 March 1785.*

First movement: ***Allegro maestoso** (maestoso* = **"majestic"***)*

A quiet marching tune (A) **[T4/i1, 0:00]** consists of two answering phrases ("on tiptoes"): an approving sigh from the violins, and a soft, welcoming fanfare **[T4/i1, 0:11]** from the winds, brass, and timpani, with the "sigh" and the "fanfare" each repeated once. Now the full orchestra blares out its greeting **[T4/i1, 0:20]**, with the march tune in the lower strings and bassoon, and a kind of countermelody above. The music pushes forward to a climax, from which strings and winds, suddenly soft again, tumble down the scale to a resting point. Now, brass and winds start a question-and-answer encounter (B) **[T4/i1, 0:46]**, which also tumbles down the scale at the end of each phrase.

The march theme (A) returns **[T4/i1, 1:00]**, passes among the strings in imitative counterpoint, then is gradually taken up by the winds and brass as well, ever louder until the full orchestra offers a closing theme (C) **[T4/i1, 1:14]**, punctuated by a sort of fanfare from the brass and timpani. This throttles down to another, quieter theme (D) **[T4/i1, 1:28]**, set as a call-and-response session between winds and strings and rounded off with yet another appearance of theme (A) as a conversation between the "military" band (winds, brass, and timpani) and the strings **[T4/i1, 1:49]**. The definitive cadence at the

end of all this [T4/i2, 1:56] leaves no doubt but that the ritornello has
come to its end and that the soloist is ready to enter from the wings,
but Mozart inserts a darling little "bridge" theme (E) to lead the listener across. And when the soloist does make the long-delayed
entrance [T4/i2, 2:07], it is with a suspenseful teaser, a sustained
anticipatory chord that calls for a cadenza.

Under the pianist's long trill, the strings present theme (A) in
its "tiptoe" version [T4/i2, 2:24] but with the piano taking the second
phrase (what was previously called the "approving sigh" for the violins) and continuing on as the orchestra once again softly breathes its
welcoming fanfare. A new theme (F) [T4/i2, 2:42] leads the music
onward, heading toward the expected key of G for the contrasting
second theme. Before it gets there, however, a roadblock is encoun-
tered: an episode, not in the anticipated G major but, instead, in G
minor, a key Mozart frequently used to signify a kind of epic
tragedy—as in the *Symphony No. 40* and the *G-minor String Quintet.*
Here, the tragedy is short-lived: a calling-to-arms arpeggio [T4/i3,
3:12] that is answered with a prophecy (G) of the music that begins
the *Symphony No. 40* of three years later. But then the mood of the
minor key is almost immediately dispelled, dissolved in a series of
piano runs that lead to the "proper" key of G major.

The new theme (H) [T4/i4, 3:48] provides a beautiful foil to the
tiptoe march tune: a shapely, flowing sequence of descending eighth-
notes and a rounding-off phrase of greater rhythmic variety. It comes

in first in the piano; when the orchestra picks it up [T4/i4, 3:57], the piano approvingly echoes the end of each phrase then burbles onward to a reprise of theme (A). This now spreads through the orchestra, with the piano continuing its flowing motion. Suddenly [T4/i4, 4:29], the pianist remembers a fragmentary phrase from the orchestral ritornello (just before 0:46), which now comes in handy to inaugurate a series of simple melodic patterns, a dialogue between the piano and orchestra, that sweeps forward in a breathtaking display of melodious prodigality until the traditional trill from the piano brings this section to a close.

The orchestra takes over in full force [T4/i5, 5:36] with music built around themes (C) and (D), which had ended the orchestral ritornello. The music moves in and out of harmonic shadows, with the piano temporarily on the sidelines. But not for long: it returns [T4/i5, 6:25] with a new theme (I) of somewhat downcast mien. Winds and strings pick up the new tune [T4/i5, 6:40], with stern rejoinders from the piano. The argument becomes more heated [T4/i5, 7:17] as piano and orchestra seemingly pursue each other from one key to the next and then [T4/i5, 7:40] settle back in a long meditation, out of which comes the definite sense that the music is heading back toward a recapitulation of familiar material in its proper key.

That happens, finally [T4/i6, 7:54], with the orchestra presenting its march tune and the answering fanfare, first soft and then full volume, mostly as it had at the start of the movement. Mostly, but not entirely: at **[T4/i6, 8:30]**, the orchestra and piano take up theme (A) rather quietly but in what appears to be the wrong key—F major instead of C. A little arithmetic will explain this disparity: in the exposition, Mozart began in the key of C and landed in G for the second theme—up five steps, in other words. Now, in the recapitulation—part of whose function is to steer the listener back to the original key—Mozart skews the action around to F, and when he goes up those five steps he will land on the hoped-for C. Clever? It's a musical reworking of the old issue of lowering the bridge as opposed to raising the river. In any case, the ruse worked, as usual (at least in Mozart's hands): theme (H) returns in C major **[T4/i6, 9:00]**, with the echoes from the piano as before, and this leads to another long, serene dialogue, with theme (A) tossed from strings to winds and the piano rippling along in accordance.

But one of the composer's jobs is to keep the almost-literal repeat of his material, in the recapitulation of a sonata-form movement, from sounding *too* literal, and Mozart's bag of tricks in this regard is truly amazing. Now **[T4/i7, 10:07]**, he brings back an episode from the ritornello (at 0:46), the dialogue between the brass and the woodwinds (B) that he has carefully withheld all this time to make its delayed return sound that much fresher. It does, first in its original scoring, then for piano. Mozart then returns to the order of events from the exposition—in, of course, the key of C. The piano skitters through its prodigal sequence of melodic gambits [T4/i7, 10:05]; the orchestra bursts into the action [T4/i7, 11:00] with an emphatic restatement of theme (A), leading to a full stop [T4/i7, 11:20] for the customary cadenza. The orchestra resumes the action [T4/i8, 12:48] with a reprise of the music that ended the ritornello, adding a whole new melodic twist [T4/i8, 13:15] in the very last four bars.

The sequence of events:

Ritornello	Exposition	Development	Recapitulation	Cadenza	Coda
A-B-A-C-D-A-E	A-F-G-H-A	C+D+E-I	A-H-B-A	A+H	A

Beyond its extraordinary fund of wit and sheer beauty, this first movement is a remarkable demonstration of the freedom Mozart assumed in dealing with classical structural principles. Basically, it follows the "rules:" a ritornello forecasting the material of the movement (or some of it, anyway); the exposition that starts off in the tonic key and moves to the dominant key; the development moving through many keys; the recapitulation retracing the material of the exposition without the key-change; a cadenza and a short closing. But Mozart constantly stretches these rules; his choices of what should and should not be repeated seem to stem from an exquisite sense of balance. Some of the material from the exposition (themes F and G) never does return, nor does the startling G-minor episode (G); a theme not previously heard (I) occupies most of the development;

the recapitulation includes the long-lost theme (C) that was heard in the ritornello but not since.

Second movement: *Andante*

In these loosenings of traditional practice, Mozart stands on the brink of a new musical era, romanticism, in which personal expression becomes more important and the symmetries and balances of classicism less so. If any single work confirms this position, it must be the extraordinary slow movement of this concerto. It was made famous by its use in a melancholy Swedish love epic called *Elvira Madigan;* those who know the music on its own, however, rise up in horror at the way it is faded in and out time and again in the film—this flowing, seamless, wordless song that seems to consist of a single uninterrupted breath.

The first violins begin the sublime melody (A) [T5/i1, 0:00] over a throbbing triplet accompaniment in second violins and violas and a steady pizzicato (plucking of strings) tread in cellos and basses. All the violins and violas are muted (by the insertion of a comblike gadget over the strings that damps the sound), giving the music a veiled, moonlit character. The throbbing triplets appear, either in the orchestra or the piano, in all but three of the movement's 104 measures; the pizzicato tread is, likewise, almost constantly present. One begins to hear this steady, featureless accompaniment as a nocturnal landscape across which strands of moonlight seem to move. The very irregularity of the movement—themes in the "wrong" order or in the "wrong" key—contributes to the continuity.

Despite its sense of unbroken flow, theme (A) embraces several distinctive phrases that sometimes appear by themselves. The first (A_1) **[T5/i1, 0:27]** is marked by extremely wide skips, an operatic device that adds to the songlike quality of this melody. The second (A_2) **[T5/i1, 0:41]** is also vocal in character, a kind of leaning upward into a dissonant note (think of the first notes of the "Love Theme" from Tchaikovsky's *Romeo and Juliet*). The third (A_3) **[T5/i1, 1:01]** is a flowing, rounding-off kind of theme. The piano repeats the sequence **[T5/i1, 1:24]** through (A), (A_1), and the start of (A_2), then breaks off **[T5/i1, 2:15]** for a short journey through minor keys before returning to (A_2) **[T5/i1, 2:46]**, with poignant sighs from the woodwinds, and (A_3) **[T5/i1, 3:02]**.

A cloud passes across the landscape **[T5/i2, 3:23]**. Still, over the triplets and the pizzicato, the music flows through a sequence of minor keys, with a tiny, new idea (B) beholden to the wide skips of (A_1) **[T5/i2, 3:49]** that leads, through some marvelously slippery harmony **[T5/i2, 4:19]**, to an expectant half-cadence, at the only spot in the movement where the triplets' throbbing ceases—for only three measures **[T5/i2, 4:25]**. Theme (A) re-enters **[T5/i3, 4:31]**; it has the feeling of a recapitulation, but it's in a "wrong" key (A-flat instead of F). It continues to drift harmonically, and when it finally arrives at the home key, it does so with (A_2) **[T5/i3, 5:07]** in a somewhat ornamented version. Now (A_1) returns **[T5/i3, 5:50]** out of sequence, but serving as an eloquent peroration, with new flashes of soft color from the winds. Toward the very end **[T5/i3, 6:11]**, a closing theme seems, like the music itself, to vanish in the distance.

Third movement: *Allegro vivace assai* ("rather lively")

The opening theme (A) of this final movement **[T6/i1, 0:00]** is close in spirit to the opening of the first movement, even to the extent of rounding off the phrases with a small flourish from winds, brass, and timpani. The first part of the theme, not much more than an up-and-down pitter-patter in eighth notes, repeats and then moves on to a momentary pause, sufficiently pregnant in that the soloist is expected to provide a cadenza **[T6/i1, 0:20]**, which ends **[T6/i1, 0:29]** with a recall of theme (A). The orchestra plays a closing theme **[T6/i1, 0:34]**: strings first, then the winds in a delicious passage **[T6/i1, 0:46]** that evokes images of toy soldiers. The piano returns with what sounds like a tune of its own **[T6/i1, 0:55]**, but this soon blends into a reprise of (A) and moves on to the contrasting key of G with a truly new theme (B) **[T6/i2, 1:32]**, brought on in that wind-serenade scoring that Mozart has used before to tickle the ears and answered by the piano. A closing theme (C) **[T6/i2, 2:03]** reverses the sequence: piano first, then winds.

Theme (A) returns, beginning with the piano **[T6/i3, 2:21]** as it did at [0:29], again rounded off by the orchestra **[T6/i3, 2:51]**. It then starts to drift through several keys, in the guise of a development, with some interesting piano scoring that sends the theme down to the player's left hand [T6/i3, 3:39]. Eventually the music comes home to C major [T6/i4, 4:05] and repeats the order of former events in a fairly normal pattern: 4:19=0:55; 4:33=1:32; 5:24=2:03, breaking off for a cadenza [T6/i5, 5:24]. Finally, the charming and quirky theme (A) returns for one last blithe sail across the horizon, a journey that is cut short by a couple of whomps from the orchestra.

Basic Mozart
The Essential Recordings

1 ***Piano Concerto No. 20 in D minor,*** K. 466; ***Piano Concerto No. 21 in C,*** K. 467. Alfred Brendel, pianist, with Sir Neville Marriner conducting The Academy of St. Martin-in-the-Fields. Taken from Philips 420 867-2 and Philips 400 028-2.

See the Play by Play chapter for a detailed journey through these works.

2 ***Symphony No. 40 in G minor,*** K. 550; and ***No. 41 in C "Jupiter,"*** K. 551. John Eliot Gardiner conducting the English Baroque Soloists. Philips 426-315-2.

The summer of 1788 found Mozart aware of his worsening physical condition, desperate for money (as his begging letters to his friends attest) and fearful also that his tenuous hold on the affections of the Viennese public was beginning to erode. He had no major commissions, yet he feverishly set about composing a set of three symphonies—the only ones he created in Vienna—hoping to present them sometime later at a subscription concert that might raise some much-needed cash. That concert never happened; one of the symphonies—probably *No. 40*—may have been read through at a concert by the Tonkunstler Society of Vienna, almost three years after its completion. There is no substantial evidence of this, or of performances of the other two symphonies during Mozart's lifetime. Like Franz Schubert a generation later, Mozart may very well have gone to his grave without hearing his greatest symphonies.

The three works present an extraordinary sweep across orchestral styles in the last years of classicism: *No. 39* with its exuberant winds and trumpets declaring the richness of its own tone-color; *No. 41* with its amazing contrapuntal finale, its brilliant brass proclamations and its slow movement that seems set in some mystical twilight, with harmonic turns that catch in the listener's throat. *No. 40* probes the essence of tragedy and seems to map the way to salvation through endurance. Like only one other of Mozart's orchestral works—the *Concerto No. 24* (K. 491)—it ends as it began, in a minor key, ignoring the classical principle of the requisite happy ending. It is one of those few works of Western art to which the ideal of perfection applies.

This performance is by an ensemble of period instruments: strings, winds, and brass constructed to reproduce the designs of

Mozart's own time. The *Symphony No. 40* played is Mozart's second version, in which he added the warm, caressing tones of clarinets to his original instrumentation.

Tracks 1-4:

Symphony No. 40 in G minor

Track 1:

Molto allegro

Sonata form

- 0:00 Exposition: first theme
- 0:31 First theme (variation)
- 0:48 Second theme
- 1:17 First theme (brief variation)
- 1:33 Third theme
- 1:46 First theme (return)
- 2:13 First theme (return of variation)
- 2:31 Second theme (return)
- 3:15 Third theme (return)
- 3:29 Development: first theme
- 4:32 Recapitulation: first theme
- 4:59 First theme (variation)
- 5:36 Second theme
- 6:25 Third theme
- 6:34 Coda

Track 2:

Andante

Sonata form

- 0:00 Exposition: first theme
- 1:07 Second theme
- 2:02 Third theme
- 3:01 First theme (repeat)
- 4:05 Second theme (repeat)
- 5:01 Third theme (repeat)
- 5:56 Development: first theme
- 7:06 Recapitulation: first theme
- 8:33 First theme (variation)
- 8:57 Third theme
- 9:54 First theme (repeat)
- 10:49 First theme (repeat of variation)
- 11:02 First theme (return of repeat)
- 12:54 Third theme (repeat)

Track 3:

Menuet and trio

0:00 Menuet: first part

0:33 Second part

1:36 Trio: first part

2:20 Second part

3:18 Menuet: first part (repeat)

3:50 Second part (repeat)

Track 4:

Finale: Allegro assai

Sonata form

0:00 Exposition: first theme

1:02 Second theme

1:29 Third theme

1:50 First theme (repeat)

2:51 Second theme (repeat)

3:19 Third theme (repeat)

3:39 Development: first theme

4:52 Recapitulation: first theme

5:27 Second theme

5:54 Third theme

6:22 First theme (development)

7:35 First theme (repeat)

8:10 Second theme (repeat)

8:37 Third theme (repeat)

Tracks 5-8:

Symphony No. 41 ("Jupiter") in C

Track 5:

Allegro vivace

Sonata form

0:00 Exposition: first theme

1:32 Second theme

2:45 Third theme

3:15 First theme (repeat)

4:45 Second theme (repeat)

5:56 Third theme (repeat)

6:27 Development: third theme

7:28 First theme

8:00 Third theme (return)

8:11 Recapitulation: first theme

9:41 Second theme

10:51 Third theme

Track 6:

Andante cantabile

Sonata form

0:00 Exposition: first theme

1:25 Second theme

2:07 Third theme

3:22 First theme (repeat)

4:44 Second theme (repeat)

5:28 Third theme (repeat)

6:48 Development: second theme

7:30 Third theme

7:49 Recapitulation: first theme

8:45 Second theme

8:58 Third theme

10:07 Coda (based on first theme)

4:39 Development: first theme

5:39 Recapitulation: first theme

6:21 Second theme

7:15 Third theme

8:35 First theme (repeat)

9:16 Second theme (repeat)

10:15 Third theme (repeat)

Track 7:
Menuet and trio

0:00 Menuet: first part

0:35 Second part

2:08 Trio: first part

2:26 Second part

3:10 Menuet: first part (repeat)

3:45 Second part (repeat)

Track 8:
Finale: Allegro molto

0:00 Exposition: first theme

1:06 Second theme

2:00 Third theme (variation of first theme)

2:19 First theme (repeat)

3:24 Second theme (repeat)

4:19 Third theme (repeat)

3 **Serenade in G** ("Eine kleine Nachtmusik"), K. 525; **Sextet in F** ("Ein musikalischer Spass"), K. 522; **Divertimento in D,** K. 136. The Academy of St. Martin-in-the-Fields Chamber Ensemble. Philips 412 269-2.

It is almost, if not quite, true that Mozart was incapable of writing a dull work. Surely the level of quality and delight in even the incidental pieces tossed off as background music at aristocratic dinners and dances—works variously called "Divertimento," "Serenade," or simply "Night Music"—is remarkably high. We don't know the specific circumstances for which these three works were composed; we do know the music, which ought to suffice. The early *Divertimento* is one of a set of three composed by the sixteen-year-old Mozart in Salzburg; full of sweetness and charm, it is a clear mirror of the rococo style of its time, out of which Mozart would soon emerge. The "Night Music" and the "Musical Joke" are works that mark Mozart's maturity; the first, elegantly and beautifully formed (and with a startling harmonic shift in the development of the first movement that lets us know that this is music to take seriously). The "Joke" is just that, a merciless parody on second-rate composers who write themselves into holes, indulge in disastrous dead-end improvisations and, at the conclusion, come totally unglued in a free-for-all of ineptitude. Mozart undoubtedly knew many composers of this level of proficiency; their descendants are still among us. You can tell them easily; they're the ones who refer to K. 525 as (ugh!) "the Eine Kleine."

Tracks 1-4:

Eine kleine Nachtmusik

Track 1:
Allegro

Sonata form

0:00 Exposition: first theme

0:50 Second theme

1:40 Exposition (repeat): first theme

2:28 Second theme

3:17 Development: first theme

3:25 Second theme

3:52 Recapitulation: first theme

4:38 Second theme

5:33 Coda

Track 2:
Romanze

0:00 First theme

2:00 Second theme

3:03 First theme (partial)

3:33 Third theme

4:23 First theme (return)

5:22 Coda, based on first theme

Track 3:
Menuet

0:00 Menuet

0:44 Trio

1:40 Menuet: repeat

Track 4:
Rondo

Rondo form

0:00 First theme

0:23 Second theme

0:38 First theme (variation)

1:24 Second theme (return)

1:40 First theme (repeat of variation)

2:30 Second theme (return)

2:45 First theme (repeat of variation)

3:25 Coda, based on first theme

Tracks 5-7:

Divertimento

Track 5:
Allegro

Sonata form

0:00 Exposition: first theme

0:22 Second theme

1:06 Exposition (repeat): first theme

1:28 Second theme

2:11 Development: first theme

3:02 Recapitulation: first theme

3:23 Second theme

Track 6:
Andante

Ternary form ABA

0:00 A: first part

1:22 Second part

2:06 B: first part

2:33 A: first part (repeat)

3:53 Second part (repeat)

Track 7:
Presto

Ternary form ABA

0:00 A: first part

0:44 First part: repeat

1:28 B: first part (canon)

1:49 A: first part (return)

Tracks 8-11:

Ein musikalische Spass

Track 8:
Allegro

Sonata form

0:00 Exposition: first theme

0:31 Second theme

0:52 Exposition (repeat): first theme

1:22 Second theme

1:44 Development: first theme

2:13 Recapitulation: first theme

2:38 Second theme

2:52 Coda, based on first theme

3:13 Development (repeat): first theme

3:42 Recapitulation (repeat): first theme

4:08 Second theme

4:22 Coda: repeat

Track 9:
Menuet and trio

0:00 Menuet: first part

0:42 Second part

1:29 Second part: repeat

2:13 Trio: first part

3:23 Second part

4:10 Second part: repeat

5:03 Menuet (repeat): first part

5:22 Second part

Track 10:
Andante cantabile

Sonata form

0:00 Exposition: first theme

0:43 Second theme

1:07 Third theme

1:45 Development: first theme

2:46 Recapitulation: first theme (in minor)

3:41 Second theme

4:00 Third theme (partial)

4:54 Cadenza: with violin

5:49 Third theme (remainder)

Track 11:
Presto

Sonata form

0:00 Exposition: first theme

0:28 Second theme (fugue)

1:07 Third theme

1:37 First theme (return)

1:45 Development: first theme

2:01 Recapitulation: first theme

2:15 Second theme

3:00 Third theme

3:26 First theme (return)

3:38 Coda, based on first theme

4:03 Cadenza (sequence of keys)

4 **_Requiem,_** K. 626. Arleen Auger, soprano; Cecilia Bartoli, mezzo-soprano; Vinson Cole, tenor; René Pape, bass; Sir Georg Solti conducting the Vienna State Opera Choir and Vienna Philharmonic Orchestra. London 433-688-2.

This recording was made on 5 December 1991, the 200th anniversary of Mozart's death, in Vienna's Stefansdom, the site of the composer's funeral service. Included are the commemorative prayers spoken to celebrate the occasion. The edition is by the classical scholar H. C. Robbins Landon, incorporating the "completions" of the work by Mozart's pupils Franz Xaver Süssmayr, Josef Eybler, and Franz Jakob Freystädtler. Arguments over the authenticity of various versions of the great unfinished Requiem go on, but all you really need is to hear the stabbing dissonance by the chorus at its first entrance, surrounded by the harrowing bleakness of the low wood-winds to render meaningless any further debate. The problems of what music is by Mozart and what is by his students is complicated by statements that Constanze made in later years. Some of her scenarios have the composer practically finishing the score himself, dictating only the final details at his bedside; other tales imply there were great gaping holes that the students needed to fill in. One thing is certain, however: the canard perpetuated in _Amadeus,_ both play and film, whereby the dying Mozart dictates the music to, of all unlikely people, Salieri, is both poor history and lousy theater.

Track 1:

Introitus (Requiem eternam) *(Chorus/soprano solo)*

0:35 First theme: D minor

1:21 First theme: chorus "Requiem"

2:37 Second theme: soprano solo "Te decet hymnus" B flat major

3:52 First theme: chorus (return)

Track 2:

Kyrie (Chorus)

Fugue

0:00 First theme: basses "Kyrie" D minor

0:02 Second theme: altos "Christe"

0:10 First theme: sopranos

0:12 Second theme: tenors

2:09 Text painting "Kyrie": full chorus

Track 3:

Dies Irae (Chorus)

0:00 First theme: "Dies irae" D minor

0:16 Second theme: "Quantus tremor" F major

0:37 First theme: A minor

0:51 Second theme: C minor

1:08 Text painting "Quantus": A minor

1:36 Third theme: "Cuncta stricte" D minor

Track 4:

Tuba mirum (Solo quartet)

0:00 First entrance: bass "Tuba mirum" B flat major

0:48 Second entrance: tenor "Mors stupebit" F minor

1:32 Third entrance: alto "Judex ergo" D minor

1:49 Fourth entrance: soprano "Quid" B flat major

2:20 Text painting "Cum vix justus": quartet

Track 5:

Rex Tremendae (Chorus)

0:00 First theme: orchestra/chorus "Rex" G minor

0:30 Text painting: "Rex tremendae"

1:19 Second theme: "Salva me"

Track 6:
Recordare (Solo quartet)

0:00 First theme: orchestra

0:28 First theme: alto/bass "Recordare" F major

0:41 First theme: soprano/tenor "Quod sum causa"

0:55 Second theme: bass/quartet "Ne me perdas"

1:21 Third theme: quartet "Quaerens me"

1:56 First theme: soprano/tenor "Juste" B flat major

2:11 Second theme: quartet "Ante diem"

2:37 Fourth theme: quartet "Ingemisco"

3:28 First theme: alto/bass "Preces meae" (return) F major

4:07 Second theme: quartet "Inter oves"

Track 7:
Confutatis (Chorus)

0:00 First theme: tenors/basses "Confutatis" A minor

0:17 Second theme: sopranos/altos "Voca me" C major

0:30 Text painting "Confutatis": tenors/basses sequence through various keys

0:48 Second theme: soprano/altos (return)

1:18 Third theme: full chorus "Oro supplex"

Track 8:
Lacrymosa (Chorus)

0:00 First theme: orchestra D minor

0:13 First theme: chorus "Lacrymosa"

0:52 First theme: chorus A minor

1:29 Second theme: chorus "Huic ergo"

2:12 First theme: chorus "Dona eis"

Track 9:
Offertorium (Domine Jesu) (Chorus/solo quartet)

0:00 First theme: chorus "Domine Jesu" G minor

0:17 Second theme: chorus "De poenis inferni" B flat major

0:40 First theme: chorus "Libera me" A flat major

0:57 Third theme: chorus "Ne absorbeat" (short fugue)

1:28 First theme (variation): solo quartet "Sed signifer"

2:01 Fourth theme: chorus "Quam olim Abrahae" G minor

Track 10:
Hostias (Chorus)

0:00 First theme: "Hostias"

0:43 Text painting "Hostias": B flat minor/D flat major/F major

1:27 First theme (variation): "Fac eas"

1:51 Fourth theme (of Track 9): chorus "Quam olim Abrahae" (return)

Tracks 11, 12:
Spoken prayers

Track 13:
Sanctus (Chorus)

0:00 First theme: "Sanctus" D major

0:28 Second theme: "Pleni sunt coeli"

0:52 Third theme: "Osanna" (short fugue) D major

Track 14:
Benedictus (Solo quintet/chorus)

0:00 First theme: orchestra B flat major

0:14 First theme: alto/quartet "Benedicimus"

1:21 Second theme: orchestra F major

1:41 Text painting "Benedictus": bass/quartet (return)

2:02 First theme: bass/quartet (return)

3:59 Third theme: chorus "Osanna" B flat major (short fugue)

Tracks 15, 16:
Spoken prayers

Track 17:
Agnus Dei (Chorus)

0:00 First theme: "Agnus Dei" D minor

0:26 Second theme: "Dona eis" F major

0:48 First theme: F major

1:10 Second theme: G major

1:40 First theme: C major

2:00 Second theme: B flat major

Track 18:

Communio (Te decet hymnus)

(Soprano solo/chorus)

- **0:00** Second theme (from Track 1): soprano solo "Te decet" B flat major
- **1:26** First theme (from Track 1): chorus "Requiem" D minor
- **2:57** First theme (from Track 2): chorus "Cum sanctis" D minor
- **3:01** Second theme (from Track 2): chorus "Cum sanctis"

5 *Piano Sonatas in C,* K. 330; *in A,* K. 331; *in F,* K. 332; *Sonata in E-flat*, K. 282. London 417 817-2.

The best of Mozart's solo piano music was composed for his own performance or for the instruction of his pupils. The early *E-flat Sonata* begins with a sweet, tender almost-song for the pianist, prophetic of the way the mature composer learned to impart a "vocal" style to the instruments. Even more charming, however, is the *A-major Sonata,* composed in Salzburg and astounding its listeners with its famous rondo in the so-called "Turkish" style. The exotic Middle East fascinated eighteenth-century audiences; a particular kind of music, set in a sing-song minor mode, seemed to typify that world. Mozart dabbled in it twice, in the finale of his *A-major Violin Concerto* (K. 218) and in this rondo. Later, in his opera *The Abduction from the Seraglio,* he turned Turkish with a vengeance, adding the jangles of triangle and cymbals to his orchestra to fill in the picture of the Pasha Selim and his harem.

Tracks 1-3:

Sonata in C

Track 1:

Allegro moderato

Sonata form

0:00 Exposition: first theme

0:34 Second theme

1:14 Third theme

1:44 Exposition (repeat): first theme

2:14 Second theme

2:56 Third theme

3:25 Development

4:17 Recapitulation: first theme

4:48 Second theme

5:30 Third theme

5:57 Coda (based on development)

Track 2:
Andante cantabile

Ternary form ABA

0:00 A: first theme

0:29 First theme: repeat

0:59 Second theme

1:44 Second theme: repeat

2:30 B: first theme

3:00 First theme: repeat

3:29 Second theme

3:57 Second theme: repeat

4:25 First theme (partial return)

4:42 A: first theme

5:11 Second theme

5:56 Coda (based on first theme of B)

Track 3:
Allegretto

Sonata form

0:00 Exposition: first theme

0:45 Second theme

1:04 Third theme

1:35 Exposition (repeat): first theme

2:20 Second theme

2:40 Third theme

3:11 Development

3:51 Recapitulation: first theme

4:40 Second theme

5:00 Third theme

Tracks 4-6:

Sonata in A

Track 4:
Andante grazioso

Theme and variations

0:00 Theme: first part

0:25 First part: repeat

0:50 Second part

1:22 Second part: repeat

1:53 Variation I: first part

2:13 First part: repeat

2:33 Second part

3:02 Variation II: first part

3:23 First part: repeat

3:43 Second part

4:12 Variation III: first part

4:40 First part: repeat

5:07 Second part

5:44 Variation IV: first part

6:07 First part: repeat

6:30 Second part

7:01 Variation V: first part (Adagio)

7:49 First part: repeat

8:36 Second part

9:45 Variation VI: first part (Allegro)

9:59 First part: repeat

10:12 Second part

Track 5:
Menuet and trio

ABA form

0:00 Menuet: first theme

0:29 First theme: repeat

0:59 Second theme

1:20 First theme: repeat

1:52 Trio: first theme

2:17 First theme: repeat

2:42 Second theme

3:40 Second theme: repeat

4:38 Menuet (repeat): first theme

5:08 Second theme

Track 6:
Allegretto "Alla Turca"

0:00 First theme

0:43 Second theme

0:58 Third theme

1:41 Second theme: return

1:56 First theme: return

2:25 Second theme: variation

2:40 Coda

Tracks 7-9:

Sonata in F

Track 7:
Allegro

Sonata form

0:00 Exposition: first theme

0:31 Second theme

0:55 Third theme

1:37 Fourth theme

2:08 Exposition (repeat): first theme

2:39 Second theme

3:03 Third theme

3:44 Fourth theme

4:16 Development: based on first
       theme

4:38 Material from third theme

5:12 Recapitulation: first theme

5:43 Second theme

6:12 Third theme

6:54 Fourth theme

Track 8:

Adagio

Binary form AB

0:00 A: first theme

0:27 First theme (in minor)

0:55 Second theme

1:22 Second theme: repeat

1:45 Third theme

2:15 B: first theme (variation)

2:41 First theme (in minor with variation)

3:09 Second theme (with variation)

4:02 Third theme (with variation)

Track 9:

Allegro assai

Sonata form

0:00 Exposition: first theme, Part I

0:16 First theme, Part II

0:42 Second theme, Part I

0:59 Second theme, Part II

1:17 Third theme

1:46 Exposition (repeat): first theme, Part I

2:02 First theme, Part II

2:29 Second theme, Part I

2:45 Second theme, Part II

3:03 Third theme

3:32 Development, based on first theme

4:39 Recapitulation: first theme, Part I

4:55 First theme, Part II

5:04 Second theme, Part I

5:22 Second theme, Part II

5:41 Third theme

6:12 Coda, based on first theme, Part I

Tracks 10-12:

Sonata in E flat

Track 10:

Adagio

Sonata form

0:00 Exposition: introduction

0:22 First theme

0:57 Second theme

1:24 Exposition (repeat): introduction

1:44 First theme

2:19 Second theme

2:45 Development, based on second theme

3:19 Recapitulation: first theme

3:57 Second theme

4:23 Coda, based on introduction

Track 11:
Two menuets

0:00 Menuet I: first part

0:36 Second part

1:02 Second part: repeat

1:34 Menuet II: first part

1:59 First part: repeat

2:23 Second part

3:01 Second part: repeat

3:39 Menuet I (repeat): first part

3:56 Second part

Track 12:
Allegro

Binary form

0:00 First part

0:34 First part: repeat

1:08 Second part

2:05 Second part: repeat

6 *Concertos for Horn and Orchestra: No. 1 in D,* K. 412; *No. 2 in E-flat,* K. 417; *No. 3 in E flat,* K. 447; *No. 4 in E flat,* K. 495. Barry Tuckwell, soloist and conductor, with the English Chamber orchestra. London 410 284-2.

In Vienna, Mozart made the acquaintance of a certain Ignaz Leutgeb (or Leitgeb), a fellow Salzburger who had come to the city in 1777, opened a cheese shop, and became a sensationally gifted horn player on the side. He begged Mozart to compose for him, and was rewarded with a repertory that would make any brass player jealous: three full-length works plus two movements for another one. (That two-movement work, known as *No. 1* and actually patched together from movements composed at different times, may actually date from later than the other three; does it matter?)

The three complete works are all in E flat, the most comfortable key for Leutgeb's valveless "natural" or hunting horn. (Barry Tuckwell, however, uses the modern horn with valves, although he claims it's no easier to play than the older model.) The concertos belong alongside, if ever so slightly below, the piano concertos in demonstrating Mozart's wonderful gift for getting wordless instruments to sing. Listen, for example, to the ineffably lovely tune in the slow movement of *No. 3;* it could be an outtake from some of the Countess' music in Figaro. Mozart also allows his soloist to exploit the familiar hunting horn-calls in the finales of all the works.

Mozart must have had a firm affection for the skilled, if socially clumsy hornist/cheesemonger; his scores are full of witty, if not entirely civilized, greetings to "that ass, ox and fool of a Leutgeb." The music itself is sufficient evidence of his high regard for his old pal from back home.

Tracks 1-2:

Concerto No. 1 in D

Track 1:

Allegro

Sonata form

- 0:00 Exposition: first theme: orchestra
- 0:25 Second theme: orchestra
- 0:43 First theme: with horn
- 1:15 Third theme: with horn
- 1:59 First theme (development): orchestra
- 2:40 First theme (development): with horn
- 3:11 Recapitulation: first theme: with horn
- 3:48 Third theme: orchestra
- 3:59 Second theme: orchestra, then with horn

Track 2:

Rondo (Allegro)

Rondo form

- 0:00 First theme: orchestra
- 0:12 First theme: with horn
- 0:24 Second theme: Orchestra, then with horn
- 0:54 First theme (return)
- 1:27 Third theme
- 2:00 Fourth theme
- 2:11 First theme (return)
- 2:46 Fifth theme
- 3:01 First theme (final return)

Tracks 3-5:

Concerto No. 4 in E flat

Track 3:

Allegro

Sonata form

- 0:00 Introduction
- 0:23 First theme: orchestra

1:00 Second theme

1:23 First theme: with horn

1:48 Second theme: with horn

2:25 First theme (return): orchestra

2:48 Third theme

3:02 Development: first theme

4:37 Recapitulation: first theme

5:02 Second theme

5:37 First theme (return)

6:26 Hom cadenza

7:13 Introduction (return)

7:27 Second theme (return)

Track 4:

Romanza

Rondo form

0:00 First theme: with horn

0:35 First theme: orchestra

1:08 Second theme

2:05 First theme (extended)

2:45 Third theme

3:47 First theme (return)

4:15 Coda

Track 5:

Allegro vivace

Rondo form

0:00 First theme

0:15 Second theme

1:04 First theme (return)

1:18 Third theme

1:53 First theme (return)

2:08 Second theme (variation)

2:50 Cadenza

3:02 First theme (variation)

Tracks 6-8:

Concerto No. 2 in E flat

Track 6:

Allegro maestoso

0:00 Exposition: first theme: orchestra

0:18 Second theme: orchestra

0:48 First theme: with horn

1:28 Second theme: with horn

3:00 Development: introduction

3:17 First theme: with horn

3:54 Recapitulation: first theme: orchestra

4:12 First theme: with horn

4:54 Second theme: orchestra, then with horn

6:06 First theme (return): orchestra

Track 7:
Andante

Rondo form

0:00 First theme (abbreviated): orchestra

0:22 First theme (complete): with horn

1:01 Second theme

1:27 First theme (return): with horn

1:54 Second theme (return)

2:43 Coda

Track 8:
Rondo (Allegro)

Rondo form

0:00 First theme

0:18 Second theme

0:54 First theme (return)

1:12 Third theme

1:50 First theme (return)

2:07 Fourth theme

2:46 First theme (variation)

Tracks 9-11:

Horn Concerto No. 3 in E flat

Track 9:
Allegro

Sonata form

0:00 Exposition: first theme: orchestra

0:19 Second theme: orchestra

0:56 First theme: with horn

1:42 Second theme: with horn

2:16 Third theme (closing material)

2:42 Development: second theme

3:42 Recapitulation: first theme

4:36 Second theme

5:41 Cadenza

6:10 Third theme

Track 10:
Romanza (Larghetto)

Rondo form

0:00 First theme

0:48 Second theme

1:21 First theme (with interlude)

2:21 Third theme

2:51 First theme (return)

3:15 Coda

Track 11:

Allegro

Rondo form

0:00 First theme

0:33 Second theme

0:50 Third theme (variation of first
       theme)

1:15 First theme (variation)

1:35 Fourth theme

2:22 First theme (return)

2:37 Third theme (interrupts)

2:56 First theme (resumption)

7 *Concerto for Clarinet and Orchestra in A,* K. 622; *Quintet for Clarinet and Strings in A*, K. 581. Erich Hoeprich, basset clarinet, with Frans Brüggen conducting members of the Orchestra of the Eighteenth Century (in the concerto) and Lucy van Dael and Alda Stuurup, violins; Wim ten Have, viola; and Wouter Möller, cello (in the quintet). Played on period instruments, with the lower-pitched "basset clarinet" close to the instrument Mozart had in mind. Philips 420-242-2.

Mozart and the clarinet came on the scene at about the same time. Eyed with some suspicion at first as a mere "band" instrument (as was its close relative, the saxophone, a century later), the clarinet made its way via the opera orchestra into the concert repertory. It is safe to say that no composer, then or since, has written for it, as soloist or as member of the orchestra, with the regard shown by Mozart. He obviously heard the instrument as the counterpart of the human voice. In *The Marriage of Figaro,* the clarinet and the Countess seem to sing with the same voice. In *Così fan tutte,* the clarinet seems to parody its own gift for passionate utterance; as the plot gets sillier, the orchestral clarinets seem to wax more poetic. And the conversations between piano and clarinet in the *Concertos Nos. 22, 23,* and *24* go beyond the need for words in expressing deep and beautiful thoughts.

Clarinetist Anton Stadler was one of Mozart's close friends during his Vienna years; for him Mozart wrote these two sublime works along with a trio for clarinet, viola, and piano. The *Clarinet Concerto* dates from Mozart's last few months; it was his last concerto. Even in the lively finale its tone is serious, even slightly tragic; significantly, for the only time in his concertos, Mozart left no room for cadenzas in any movement. Again, *Figaro*'s Countess seems to make her presence known, above all in the ethereal slow movement.

The *Quintet* moves through a greater range of moods, although once again the sublime melody of the slow movement seems to take on human form. The clarinet is not a soloist, but an equal member with the four strings; the give-and-take, in fact, is one of the wonders throughout the work. The minuet has two trios: the first is serious, with the clarinet silent; the second, by contrast, is a skittery folk dance with the clarinet in the lead. The finale is a set of variations on a tune that starts off as rather jolly and later turns into another of those haunting clarinet "arias;" then, however, the movement ends in hilarity and delight.

Tracks 1-3:

Concerto in A

Track 1:

Allegro

0:00	First theme
0:29	Second theme
0:53	First theme (variation)
1:43	Third theme
1:59	First theme: with clarinet
2:40	Fourth theme
3:30	Fifth theme
4:01	Fourth theme (return)
4:36	First theme (return)
5:29	Second theme (return)
5:50	Third theme (return)
6:05	First theme (return)
7:06	Fourth theme (return)
8:24	Second theme (return)
8:48	First theme (return)

9:28 Fourth theme (return)

10:05 Fifth theme (return)

11:13 First theme (return)

12:10 Second theme (return)

12:27 Third theme (return)

Track 2:

Adagio

Ternary form ABA

0:00 A: first theme

1:06 Second theme

1:58 B: first theme

2:42 First theme (variation)

3:45 A: first theme (return)

4:46 Second theme (return)

5:14 Coda

Track 3:

Allegro

Rondo form

0:00 First theme

0:51 Second theme

1:23 Third theme

2:04 Fourth theme

2:50 First theme (abridged variation)

3:24 Fifth theme

4:25 First theme (variation)

4:39 Third theme (return)

6:15 First theme (return)

7:07 Second theme (return)

7:36 Sixth theme

8:08 First theme (return of variation)

8:27 First theme (final return)

Tracks 4-7:

Quintet in A

Track 4:

Allegro

Sonata form

0:00 Exposition: first theme

0:40 Second theme

1:22 Third theme

2:08 Fourth theme

2:38 First theme (repeat)

3:16 Second theme (repeat)

4:00 Third theme (repeat)

4:46 Fourth theme (repeat)

5:17 Development: first theme

6:31 Recapitulation: first theme

6:49 Second theme

7:31 Third theme

8:14 Fourth theme

Track 5:

Larghetto

0:00 First theme
1:19 Second theme
1:56 Third theme
2:57 Fourth theme
3:22 First theme (return)
4:40 Second theme (return)
5:10 Coda

Track 6:

Menuet and trio

0:00 Menuet
1:28 Trio: first part
2:14 Second part
3:26 Menuet: repeat
4:09 Trio: first part: repeat
4:44 Second part: repeat
6:33 Menuet: repeat

Track 7:

Allegretto con variazioni

0:00 Theme
0:56 First variation
1:53 Second variation
2:52 Third variation
4:03 Fourth variation
4:58 Coda
5:11 Fifth variation
7:48 Coda
8:19 Sixth variation

8 ***The Marriage of Figaro,*** K. 492; highlights. Barbara Hendricks (Susanna), Lucia Popp (Countess), Agnes Baltsa (Cherubino), José van Dam (Figaro), Ruggero Raimondi (Count), Felicity Palmer (Marcellina), Robert Lloyd (Bartolo), and Neil Jenkins (Don Curzio) with Sir Neville Marriner conducting the Ambrosian Opera Chorus and the Academy of St. Martin-in-the-Fields. Philips 416 870-2.

It's easy to understand why the Viennese received *Figaro* coolly; as comedies go, it was far from the frivolous slapstick that dominated their stages in Mozart's day. *Figaro,* indeed, was a work in which—for the first time in opera—characters behaved like human beings (not always the most admirable of the breed) and where the undertones of poignant human tragedy underlaid the fun and games. The opera is supremely continuous, building up in two broad sweeps to great and complex final scenes in Acts II and IV in which the interaction among characters transpires at a breathtaking rate.

In excerpts we miss some of that, but we discover Mozart's peerless gift for defining his characters through their music: Figaro's defiant "If you want to dance I'll call the tune" set, indeed, as a dance tune with menacing steps; Bartolo's ridiculously pompous "vengeance" aria; the amorous adolescent Cherubino running out of breath as he describes his hormonal crises; the Countess, awakening to an empty bed, lamenting her lost love in the most touching terms, seconded by the rich plangence of the orchestral winds; Susanna managing to be wise and adorable at once; the Count, furious that his servants get the upper hand. It all comes down to the final scene, where everybody has teamed up with the wrong partner in the darkened garden, and in a single heavenly line of forgiveness the Countess sets things right. Listen also to the wonderful sextet midway in Act III (it was Mozart's favorite moment in the opera): Figaro reunited with his long-lost parents, the furious Susanna mistaking their embraces for the real thing, the Count nursing his wounds and the notary, the stammering Don Curzio, cheated out of the chance for a lawsuit— all at once, all indelibly etched and defined in the miracle of Mozart's vocal counterpoint.

Track 1:
Sinfonia (Overture)

0:00	First theme: strings D major
0:08	Second theme (melody): winds
0:16	First theme (return)
0:22	Second theme (return)
0:50	Third theme: A major
1:30	Fourth theme: A major
1:56	First theme (return)
2:02	Second theme (return)
3:05	Fourth theme (return): D major

Track 2:
Se vuol ballare

Bass/baritone aria, ABA "da capo" form

0:00	A: first theme: "Se vuol ballare" F major
0:43	Second theme: "Se vuol venire" C major
1:20	Third theme: "Meglio" A major
1:30	B: presto: F major
1:59	A: first theme (return)

La Vendetta

Basso aria

- **0:00** First theme: "La vendetta"
  D major
- **0:58** Second theme: "Col l'astuzia"
  E major
- **1:44** Third theme: "Se tutto"
  D major
- **2:18** First theme: "Tutto Sevilla"

Non sò più

Mezzo aria

- **0:00** First theme: "Non sò più" E flat
  major
- **0:17** Second theme: "Solo ai nomi"
  B flat major
- **0:41** First theme (return)
- **0:59** Third theme: "Parlo d'amor"
  E flat major
- **2:11** Adagio/first tempo: E flat
  major

Non più andrai

Bass/baritone aria, ABA form

- **0:00** A: first theme: "Non più
  andrai" C major
- **0:27** Second theme: "Non più avrai"
  G major
- **1:01** First theme (return)
- **1:23** Third theme: "Fra guerrieri"
- **2:17** B: text painting: "Non più
  avrai"
- **2:35** A: first theme (return)

Porgi amor

Soprano aria (through-composed)

- **0:00** Theme: orchestra
- **1:14** Theme: "Porgi amor"
- **2:29** Text painting: "Porgi amor"

Vol che sapete

Mezzo aria, ABA form

- **0:00** A: first theme: orchestra B flat
  major
- **0:19** First theme: "Voi che sapete"
- **0:46** B: second theme: "Quello"
  F major

1:22 Second theme: "Gelo" A flat
major

2:14 A: first theme (return)

Track 8:
Venite

Soprano aria (mostly through-composed)

0:00 First theme: "Venite" G major

0:34 Second theme: "La faccia"
D major

1:54 "Quel ciglio": return to G major

2:16 First theme (variation): "Se
l'amano"

Track 9:
Hai già vinta...Vedrò

Baritone aria, accompanied recitative and aria

0:00 Accompagnato: "Hai già vinta"
sequence of keys

1:27 Aria: first theme: "Vedrò"
D major

2:10 Text painting: "Vedrò"

2:49 Allegro: first theme: "Ah no!"
D major

3:29 Second theme: "Ah, che
lasciarti" G major

3:50 First theme (return)

Track 10:
Riconosci

Sextet

0:00 First theme: alto "Riconosci"
F major

0:11 First theme: bass-baritone
"Padre"

0:18 First theme: basso "Resistere"

0:25 Second theme: baritone/tenor
"E suo padre?"

0:45 Third theme: soprano "Alto,
alto" C major

1:02 First theme (variation): five
principals C major

1:17 Fourth theme: soprano/bass-
baritone "Già" C major

1:42 Fifth theme: sextet C major and
sequence of keys

2:20 First theme (variation):
alto/quintet "Lo sdegno"
F major

Track 11:
E Susanna non vien...Dove sono

Soprano accompanied recitative and aria

0:00 Accompagnato: "E Susanna"
sequence of keys

1:46 Aria: Andantino: first theme: "Dovo sono" C major

2:51 Second theme: "Perchè mai"

3:40 First theme (return)

4:32 Allegro: first theme: "Ah, se almen" G major

4:51 Second theme: same text C major

Track 12:
Sull'aria

Duet, two sopranos

0:11 First theme: "Sull'aria" B fiat major

1:40 First theme (in canon form): B flat major

Track 13:
Fandango

Spanish dance and scene

0:00 First theme: dance A minor/E minor/B major

0:47 First theme: baritone "E già" D minor

Track 14:
Aprite un po

Bass-baritone aria (basically ABA form)

0:00 First theme: "Aprire un po" F fiat major

0:22 Second theme: "Queste chiamate" B flat major

0:41 Third theme: "Son streghe" B fiat major

1:27 Fourth theme (variation of first theme): "Guardate" E flat major

Track 15:
Giunse alfin...Deh vieni

Soprano accompanied recitative and aria

0:00 Accompagnato: sequence of keys

1:16 Aria. First theme: orchestra F major

1:36 First theme "Deh vieni"

2:26 Second theme: "Qui" C major

3:07 Third theme: "Vieni, ben mio" return to F major

Track 16:
Gente, gente

Final ensemble

- **0:00** First theme: baritone "Gente, gente"
- **0:57** Second theme: soprano/tutti "Almeno" G major
- **1:21** Third theme: Andante: baritone: "Contessa"
- **3:52** Allegro assai. Tutti "Questi"

9 ***Don Giovanni,*** K. 527; highlights. Sharon Sweet (Anna), Karita Mattila (Elvira), Marie McLaughlin (Zerlina), Thomas Allen (Giovanni), Simone Alaimo (Leporello), Francisco Araiza (Ottavio), Claudio Otelli (Masetto), Robert Lloyd (Commendatore), with Sir Neville Marriner conducting the Academy of St. Martin-in-the-Fields. Philips 438-494-2.

Nothing like it had ever hit an operatic stage before: an opening scene which went from song to attempted rape to duel to murder to escape in a single uninterrupted sweep. It was a terrifying launching for an opera, and the marvel was that Mozart sustained the pace, from the horrible opening to the final moment when the murdered Commendatore returns in the form of a statue to exact revenge. The contrasts are astounding: the wily servant Leporello, tormenting the lovelorn Elvira with his "catalogo" of Giovanni's previous conquests; the folkish simplicity of the peasants celebrating Zerlina's wedding (and the slimy, compelling breakup of that simplicity as Giovanni employs music's most pleading tones to seduce the hapless girl in the opera's most famous duet). Two more aristocratic women are in Giovanni's grasp, and Mozart allots each of them a ranting, hysterical aria to vent their frustrations. And at the end, after the statue has returned to claim its retribution, the air clears as six wronged victims come forward to celebrate the defeat of their nemesis and to warn us all not to follow his evil ways.

Track 1:
Overture

0:00 Andante: first theme
("Commendatore motive")

0:40 Second theme: G minor

1:26 Third theme: sequence of keys

1:55 Allegro molto: first theme: D major

2:17 Second theme: A major

2:37 Third theme

2:58 Second theme (variation)

3:18 Third theme (variation)

3:36 First theme (variation)

3:51 Third theme (variation)

4:24 First theme (return)

4:44 Second theme (return)

5:06 Third theme (return)

5:47 Coda

Track 2:
Allegro

Soprano aria (with baritone and bass)

0:00 First theme: orchestra: E flat major

0:23 Second theme: "Ah, chi mi dice": E flat major

0:45 Third theme: "Ah, se ritrovo": B flat major

0:55 Fourth theme: "Vo farne": sequence of keys

1:09 Fifth theme: baritone: "Udisti": B flat major

1:18 Fourth theme (repeat, with interjections): "Ah, che mi"

1:48 Second theme (repeat)

2:54 Text painting: "cavare"

Track 3:
Allegro

Bass aria

0:00 Allegro: first theme: "Madamina"

0:23 Second theme: orchestra

0:42 Third theme: "Ma in Ispagna"

0:58 Fourth theme: "V'han tra": sequence of keys

1:14 Second theme (variation): "In Italia"

1:39 Third theme (variation): "Ma in"

1:51 Second theme (variation): "V'han tra"

2:10 Andante: first theme: "Nella": D major

2:54 Second theme: "Vuol d'inverno"

3:25 Third theme: "La piccina"

3:45 First theme (return): "Delle vecchie"

4:04 Fourth theme: "Sua passion"

4:42 Fifth theme: "Voi sapete"

Track 4:
Allegro

Duo and chorus

0:00 First theme: orchestra: G major

0:17 Second theme: soprano: "Giovinette"

0:33 Second theme (partial): chorus: "Ah!"

0:40 Second theme (variation): bass-baritone: "Giovinette"

0:57 Second theme (partial): chorus: "Ah!"

1:02 Third theme: duet: "Vieni"

1:13 Third theme (partial): chorus: "Ah!"

Track 5:
Andante

Soprano/baritone duet

0:00 Andante: first theme: baritone: "La ci darem": A major

0:22 First theme (variation):

soprano: "Vorrei"

0:49 Second theme: baritone: "Vieni"

1:16 First theme (return): "La ci darem"

1:42 Third theme: duet: "Vieni/Mi fai"

2:11 Allegro: first theme: "Andiam": A major

2:26 First theme (repeat)

Track 6:
Accompanied recitative

Soprano

0:00 Soprano: "Don Ottavio, son morta": sequence of keys

1:13 First theme: "Era già": E flat minor

1:43 Tempo I: "Non viene": sequence of keys

2:35 Tempo I: "Chiamo soccorso": sequence of keys

Track 7:
Andante

Soprano aria

0:00 First theme: "Or sai": D major

0:20 Second theme: "Vendetta"

0:36 Third theme: "Rammenta"

1:10 First theme (repeat): "Or sai"

1:29 Second theme (repeat): "Vendetta"

1:43 Third theme (variation): "Rammenta"

1:51 Second theme (extended variation): "Vendetta"

Track 8:

Andante sostenuto

Tenor aria

0:00 First theme: "Dalla sua pace"

1:02 Second theme: "S'ella sospira"

2:16 First theme (variation): "Dalla sua pace"

3:12 Text painting: "Dalla sua pace"

Track 9:

Presto

Baritone aria

0:00 First theme: orchestra: B flat major

0:04 First theme: "Finch'an dal vino"

0:14 Second theme: "Senz' alcun": F major

0:28 First theme (variation): "Ed io"

0:32 First theme (variation): "Finch'an"

0:40 Third theme: "Se trovi": B flat major

0:45 First theme (return): "Ah, la mia lista"

0:49 Third theme (return): "Senz' alcun"

0:56 First theme (extended return): "Ah, la mia lista"

Track 10:

Andante grazioso

Soprano aria

0:00 Andante: first theme: "Batti": F major

0:37 Second theme: "Lascierò": C major

1:24 First theme (variation): "Batti"

2:24 6/8 Allegro: first theme: "Pace, pace" F major

2:39 Text painting: "passar"

3:01 First theme (variation): "Pace, pace"

Allegro assai

Baritone/bass duet

- **0:00** First theme: "Eh via, buffone": G major
- **0:19** Second theme: "Va, che sei": D major
- **0:25** Duet (elements of both themes): "Eh via"

Andantino

Soprano/baritone/bass trio

- **0:00** First theme: soprano: "Ah, taci": A major
- **0:46** Second theme: baritone/basso: "Zitto!"
- **1:07** First theme (variation): baritone: "Elvira"
- **1:56** Third theme: baritone: "Discendi": C major
- **2:32** Fourth theme: "No, non ti credo": sequence of keys
- **3:04** First theme (extended variation): "Dei"

Allegretto

Baritone aria

- **0:00** Verse I: first theme: orchestra: D major
- **0:10** Second theme: "Deh, vieni alla finestra"
- **0:38** Third theme: "Se neghi"
- **1:00** Verse II (repeat)

Grazioso

Soprano aria

- **0:00** First theme: orchestra
- **0:16** First theme: "Vedrai, carino": C major
- **0:47** Second theme: "E lo speziale": G major
- **1:02** First theme (return): "E un certo"
- **1:39** Third theme: "Sentilo battere": C major
- **2:25** Text painting: "Sentilo"
- **2:45** First theme: final statement in orchestra

Track 15:
Andante

Sextet

0:00 Andante: first entrance: soprano: "Sola, sola": E flat major

0:32 Second entrance: bass: "Più che"

1:07 Third entrance: tenor: "Tergi": D major

1:48 Fourth entrance: soprano: "Lascia": D minor

2:27 Development: bass/soprano: "Ah, dov'è?"

2:48 Fifth entrance: quartet: "Ferma"

3:27 Development: "No, no, no!"

3:53 Sixth entrance: bass: "Perdon": C minor

4:30 Seventh entrance: quintet: "Dei, Leporello!": sequence of keys

5:09 Allegro molto: sextet: first theme: "Mille": E flat major

5:35 Second theme: basso: "Se mi salvo"

5:45 Third theme: quintet: "Che impensate"

6:00 First theme (variation): sextet: "Mille"

6:19 Second theme (repeat): bass: "Se mi salvo"

6:27 Third theme (repeat): quintet: "Che impensate"

6:55 Text painting: "Che impensate"

Track 16:
Andante grazioso

Tenor aria

0:00 First theme: orchestra: B flat major

0:19 First theme: "Il mio tesoro"

0:57 Text painting: "cercate"

1:11 Second theme: "Ditele": G minor and sequence of keys

1:41 Text painting: "tornar"

1:56 First theme (repeat): "il mio tesoro"

2:48 Second theme (variation): "Ditele"

3:09 Third theme: "Che sol"

Track 17:
Allegro assai

Accompanied recitative: Soprano

0:00 Soprano: "in quali eccessi": sequence of keys

Allegretto

Soprano aria

0:00 First theme: "Mi tradì": E flat major

0:56 Text painting: "provo"

1:09 First theme (repeat): "Mi tradì"

1:37 First theme (variation): "Quando": E flat minor

2:04 Text painting: "palpitando"

2:26 First theme (repeat): "Mi tradì"

3:11 Text painting: "Pietà"

Andante

Final scene

0:00 Introduction: orchestra (from Track 1, first theme)

0:15 First entrance: bass: "Don Giovanni!" (based on Track 1, first theme)

0:40 Second entrance: baritone: "Non l'avrei" (based on Track 1, second theme)

1:37 Third entrance: bass: "Altre" (based on Track 1, third theme)

2:02 Development: duo: "La terzana/Parla dunque"

2:31 Third entrance (variation): trio: "Parlo"

2:55 Fourth entrance: bass: "Tu m'invitasti" (based on first theme)

3:40 Development: basso: "Oibò"

4:01 Fourth entrance (variation): bass: "Risolvi"

4:44 Più stretto: first theme: baritone: "Oihmè"

5:00 Second theme (based on fourth theme): bass: "Pentiti"

5:22 Third theme (based on Track 1, first theme): bass: "Ah, tempo"

5:29 Allegro: first entrance: baritone: "Da qual": D minor

5:39 Second entrance (based on third theme): chorus/duo: "Tutto"

5:58 Second entrance (expanded repeat)

10 *The Magic Flute,* K. 620; highlights. Pilar Lorengar (Pamina), Cristina Deutekom (Queen of the Night), Renate Holm (Papagena), Stuart Burrows (Tamino), Hermann Prey (Papageno), Martti Talvela (Sarastro), Gerhard Stolze (Monostatos), with Sir Georg Solti conducting the Vienna State Opera Chorus and the Vienna Philharmonic Orchestra. London 421-302-2.

The intermingling of opposites here includes the fact that, midway in the first act, the entire opera shifts from burlesque-and-rescue to an elevated moral disquisition with comedy on the side. No matter; the immense charm of everything here makes full amends. Papageno and his magic bells eventually win the hand of Papagena, while the noble Sarastro sings music that Bernard Shaw described as "worthy for the mouth of God." The fury of the Queen of the Night is manifested in her hysterical high Fs, which lead into Sarastro's consoling super-low Es, as if that multi-octave gamut could in itself define the ups-and-downs of this strange plot and its close-to-divine music. Actually, it does.

Track 1:
Der Vogelfänger bin ich

0:00 First verse: orchestra

0:45 First verse, first theme: "Der Vogelfänger" G major

1:01 Second theme: "Weiss mit" D major

1:28 Second verse: "Der Vogelfänger"

2:12 Third verse: "Wenn alle"

Track 2:
Dies Bildnis

0:00 Introduction

0:09 First theme: "Dies Bildnis" E flat major

1:01 Second theme: "Dies Etwas"
      B flat major

2:16 Third theme: "O wenn" E flat
      major

2:47 Third theme (variation): "Ich
      würde"

3:17 First theme (variation): "Und
      Ewig"

Track 3:
O zittre nicht

0:00 Accompanied recitative:
      Introduction

0:25 Vocal entrance

1:23 Aria: larghetto: "Zum Leiden"
      G minor

3:40 Allegro moderato: "Du, du"
      B flat major

4:18 Text painting: "So sei sie dann"

Track 4:
Bei Männern

0:07 First verse: soprano: "Bei
      Männern"

0:22 Baritone: "Bei Mannern"

1:07 Second verse: soprano: "Die
      Liebe"

1:23 Baritone: "Sie würzet"

2:05 Text painting: "Mann und Weib"

Track 5:
Wie stark ist nicht

0:00 First theme: orchestra: C major

0:25 First theme: tenor: "Wie stark"

0:52 Text painting: "Wie stark"
      G major

1:23 Second theme: "Doch nur
      Pamina" C minor

2:05 Third theme: "Wo"

2:18 Brief recitative

2:29 Fourth theme: presto:
      "Veilleicht"

Track 6:
Schnelle Füsse

0:00 First entrance: duet: "Schnelle"
      G major

0:35 Second entrance: "Welche
      Freude" D major

1:05 Allegro: first entrance: tenor:
      "Ha!" G major

1:27 Second entrance: baritone:
      "Wer viel" D major

1:40 Third entrance: bells/chorus:
      "Das klinget" G major

2:20 Fourth entrance: duo: "Könnte"
      G major

Track 7:
Es lebe Sarastro

0:00 Allegro maestoso: first chorus/duo entrance: "Es lebe"

0:36 Second entrance: soprano: "Die Wahrheit"

0:56 Third entrance: chorus (return): "Es lebe"

Track 8:
Herr ich bin

0:00 Larghetto: first entrance: "Herr" F major

0:48 Second entrance: "Steh auf" G major/C major

2:05 Third entrance: "Mich rufet" C major and sequence of keys

3:12 Allegro: first entrance: "Nun" F major

3:21 Second entrance: "Er ist's" C major

4:29 Chorus (variation from track 7): "Es lebe"

5:21 Presto: chorus: "Wenn Tugend"

Track 9:
O Isis und Osiris

0:00 Introduction

0:15 First theme: "O Isis" F major

1:24 Choral response: "Stärkt" C major

1:39 Second theme (return to F major): "Lasst sie"

2:49 Choral response: "Nehmt sie" F major

Track 10:
Alles fühlt

0:00 First verse: first theme: orchestra

0:09 First theme: "Alles fühlt" C major

0:21 Second theme: "Ist mir" G major

0:29 First theme (return): "Immer" C major

0:39 Second verse

Track 11:
Der Hölle Rache

0:00 Allegro assai: "Der Hölle Rache" D minor

0:18 First theme: "Fühlt" F major

0:34 Second theme: "So bist"

0:42 Text painting: "Mehr"

1:26 Third theme: "Verstossen"
F major/G minor

1:53 Text painting: "Alle" A major

2:29 Quasi recitative: "Hört"

Track 12:
In diesen heil'gen Hallen

0:00 Introduction

0:09 First verse: first theme: "In
diesen" E major

0:50 Second theme: "Dann wandelt"

2:18 Second verse, first theme
(return): "In diesen"

3:01 Second theme (return): "Wen
solche"

Track 13:
Ach, ich fühl's

0:05 First entrance: "Ach" G minor

0:47 Second entrance: "Nimmer"
B flat major

1:38 Third entrance (development):
"Sieh, Tamino"

2:57 Fourth entrance (return to
G minor): "So wird"

Track 14:
Ein Mädchen

0:00 First verse: Andante

0:21 First entrance: "Ein Mädchen"

0:47 Allegro: first entrance: "Dann"
C major

1:01 Second entrance: "Und wie"
F major

1:94 Second verse (variation):
andante

1:39 First entrance: "Ein Mädchen"

2:04 Allegro: first entrance: "Ach
kann" C major

2:17 Second entrance: "Sonst"
F major

2:40 Third verse (variation):
andante

2:54 First entrance: "Ein Mädchen"

3:21 Allegro: first entrance: "Wird"
C major

3:34 Second entrance: "So bin ich"
F major

Track 15:
Tamino mein!

0:00 First entrance: "Tamino mein"
F major

0:33 Second entrance: "Hier sind"
F major and sequence of keys

1:31 Third entrance (quartet): "Nun komm" F major

Track 16:
Pa-pa-pa-papagena

0:01 Allegro: first theme: orchestra G major

0:10 First theme: "Pa-pa"

0:26 Second theme: "Bist du"

0:38 Third theme: "Welche Freude" D major

1:08 Fourth theme: "Erst einen" G major

1:94 Second theme (variation) "Es ist das" G major

Track 17:
Nur stille

0:00 First theme: orchestra C minor

0:10 First theme: "Nur stille"
C minor and sequence of keys

0:16 Text painting: "Nur stille"

1:23 Quartet: "Dir grosse"

1:42 Development: "Zerschmettert"

2:20 Brief accompanied recitative: "Die Strahlen"

2:48 Andante: chorus: "Heil" E flat major

3:47 Final allegro: chorus: E flat major

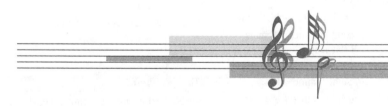

Glossary

O

Aria In Baroque and Classical opera, the action went forward in **recitative:** the singer, usually supported by a light accompaniment, vocalized in a more-or-less conversational style. Then the singer launched into an aria, a more self-contained musical episode, often in an A-B-A form, in a relatively reflective style that often ended in a virtuosic manner. Recitative: "This is what I'm doing." Aria: "This is how I feel; Why shouldn't I feel this way?; This is how I feel; Whoopee!" Without actually using the term, Mozart extended the idea of an aria into his instrumental music; the slow movements of his concertos become wordless arias.

Arpeggio The word comes from *arpa* ("harp"), and denotes a succession of notes, at least three, that outline a **harmony**. If played simultaneously, they would be a chord. Classical composers who wanted to define the **tonality** of a work at the outset often devised melodies that began by outlining the basic harmony of that tonality: e.g., the first five notes of the *Elvira Madigan* tune in the *Concerto No. 21*. The famous first prelude in Bach's *Well-Tempered Clavier, Book I* is nothing but an arpeggiated sequence of harmonies.

Chamber music   A self-explanatory concept: music meant to be played in close surroundings, in a style that's intimate and subtle. Chamber music uses only a single instrument for a part, as opposed to orchestral music where several violins, violas, or cellos may be playing in unison. The sovereign chamber-music form, from the eighteenth century to the present, is the string quartet (two violins, viola, and cello). Mozart added a second viola to give his string quintets a deeper resonance. The piano trio (piano, violin, and cello) was also a popular chamber-music medium. With every instrument given equal importance, chamber music typifies democracy in action.

Chromatic   In the most familiar harmonic system, the musical octave (from, say, C to C) is divided into twelve half-steps, also known as chromatic steps. The diatonic musical scale, which is the basis of a piece in a given **tonality**—C major, for example—is a pattern of seven tones

from those possible twelve, an arrangement of half- and whole-steps. Any other notes—an F-sharp, for instance, in the key of C—are dissonances, the alien resources a composer uses to enrich his music, the friction that makes the wheels turn. Consider the tenth note in the *Elvira Madigan* melody: it's a dissonant note within Mozart's chosen key and Mozart "milks" that dissonance as that note seems to lean heavily into the next note which, being consonant (i.e., nondissonant), is said to resolve the dissonance.

Classical   At its purest, the term refers to the ancient world. The Classical revival in the eighteenth century used ancient models (such as the Parthenon) to define its passion for clear, logical structures in all the arts, and so the term is used to describe the works of this time. Used more loosely, "Classical" also refers to music meant to be heard against a background of silence by audiences trained to applaud only at the end—as opposed to "pop."

Concerto   *Certare* means "to battle" or "to struggle"; *con* means "with."

The concerto pits small forces against large: soloist and orchestra locked in a wordless struggle. Mozart ennobled the form, turning his concertos into heartfelt "conversations" rather than merely showy pieces.

The movements of a Classical concerto follow the structural outlines of the characteristic forms of the period: sonata form, variations, rondo, etc., but with adjustments to accommodate the interplay between the soloist and the orchestra. In the typical concerto first movement (as typified by the *Concertos No. 20* and *No. 21*), the orchestra begins proceedings with a **ritornello** in which all or some of the themes of the movement are introduced. The soloist and orchestra then elaborate on this material in the **exposition.** In the **development,** the material is further dealt with, often with sudden and surprising changes of key, but the **recapitulation** brings the themes back in the more-or-less original order (with always leeway for further surprises, in Mozart's case). At the end, the orchestra comes to a complete halt, while the soloist plays a **cadenza,** a virtuosic rumination on

the themes of the movement; it was originally meant to be an improvisation (as Alfred Brendel's performance in the first and last movements of *No. 21*), but now it is generally written down. (The cadenzas for *No. 20* were composed by Beethoven.) A brief peroration, or **coda,** brings the movement to a close.

Counterpoint or **polyphony** (the terms are synonymous) Many lines of music occurring simultaneously create a contrapuntal, or polyphonic, texture. In opera, the device allows for a stageful of characters, each expressing a different thought but all woven together (as in the Act III sextet from *Figaro*). Haydn and Mozart discovered the music of Bach, the supreme contrapuntal master, late in their own careers, and were strongly impressed; the finale of Mozart's *Jupiter* Symphony, which interweaves five separate melodic lines, was one spectacular result.

Enlightenment The virtues of tolerance and brotherly love; the notion that men were born free and deserved to be free; a world view synthesizing of God, man, and nature: these were the tenets of the intellectual movement upheld by Jean Jacques Rousseau, Voltaire (a pen name for François Marie Arouet), the proponents of the Classical revival, and by such enlightened monarchs as Austria's Joseph II, who defied the excessive conservatism of Rome's church. "Enlightenment," wrote Immanuel Kant, "is a person's egress from the immaturity he had brought upon himself."

Form In the broadest sense, musical form (or structure) is the composer's way of involving a listener's memory in the unfolding of a piece. One reacts to the first music, follows a pathway to contrasting ideas, and is stirred when the initial material returns or when the composer subjects the material to variations. The greatest composers were the ones who were most successful in finding ways to stretch the meaning of form to allow for individual expression. Some of the forms they worked with were fairly simple: the rondo, for example, intersperses constant reiteration of its main theme with other contrasting sections: A-B-A-C-A-D-

A, etc. In variations, a single theme heard at the outset undergoes new complications at each return, while still clinging to its original outline. Needless to say, the examples of "pure" rondo or "pure" variations in the music of Mozart are rare; his own insights showed him ways to bend these forms in many different ways.

Harmony This refers to the ability to hear more than one tone at a time, to react to the way these simultaneous tones blend into a consonance or dissonance, and to follow the way one harmony will lead to the next to produce a progression. Dissonant harmonies set up an expectation; consonant harmonies resolve it into a feeling of arrival, and this process continues, over and over, to sweep the music to its stable, logical fulfillment.

Melody The horizontal aspect of music (as **harmony** is the vertical), the rising-falling line of expression that results from connecting the dots. Early music was nothing but melody, given a relationship to time (long notes versus short notes) by its rhythm. Other civilizations have built elaborate musical systems solely on melody; listen, for example, to the wonderful complexity of Indian classical music as played by Ravi Shankar—it is pure melody.

Movement   This is a section of a longer work (a concerto, symphony, sonata) which is musically complete in itself. In works of several movements, the composer usually arranges them to provide contrast: fast followed by slow, complex followed by simple. In Mozart's time, audiences saw nothing wrong with separating the movements of a work with other composers' music in between and, therefore, applauding at the end of each movement. Nineteenth-century composers began to see multimovement works as single expressions. Some audiences today still subscribe to the eighteenth-century practice, however.

Opera   The emergence of opera is usually dated at the start of the seventeenth century, when several Italian composers sought to "reform" music by reviving the Greek ideal of sung drama. Two centuries later, Italy remained the prime proving ground, where singers reigned supreme and sensible plots were secondary. Yet the idea of reform persisted; in the 1760s, German composer Christoph Willibald Gluck wrote music dramas that discouraged empty virtuosity in favor of serious plots abetted by serious music. After turning out a charming repertory of rather fluffy operas in the Italian style, Mozart also turned serious; one only needs to compare his *Marriage of Figaro* against the early pieces (e.g., *La finta giardiniera*) to realize what a forward step the later work represents. With his *Abduction from the Seraglio* and *Magic Flute,* he also raised the level of German opera from mere featherbrained burlesque to something musically substantial.

Sonata   It simply means "sounded" or "played," as opposed to **cantata** (which means "sung"). In Mozart's time, the sonata was a piece for one instrument (keyboard) or two (violin and piano), in several movements. Symphonies, concertos, and string quartets are members of the sonata family as well, distinguished only by the performing forces they demand.

Sonata form It could just as easily be called "symphonic" form; the term refers to the wonderfully logical and flexible organization of materials within an instrumental movement, practiced by composers in the Classical era and respected by composers of later times. The essence of the sonata form is contrast: between a first theme and melodies introduced later (the **exposition**); between one tonality and another, between a slow rate of tonality change and fast (the **development**); between the material when first heard and the subtle changes it undergoes later (the **recapitulation**). With all those variables, sonata form became a great dramatic battlefield on which Mozart could exercise with exquisite and awesome freedom. Only in the nineteenth century, by the way, was the whole notion of sonata form observed and codified by scholars. The great Classical composers never worked from rule books; they didn't need to.

Tonality (or **key**) From the Renaissance until early in the twentieth century, it was a given that Western music followed a system of tonality, defined by the succession of harmonies derived from the notes of a given scale (see **chromatic**). The tonic of the key (the note C in the key of C, for example) served as the point of origin, departure, and ultimate return; the music began in its given tonality, strayed somewhere else, and then returned, sometimes quite dramatically. The destiny of music, after the clear horizons of classicism, seems like an ongoing attempt to blur the sense of tonality; the cloudy opening of Beethoven's *Ninth Symphony* is certainly a further step in that direction, much imitated by composers later on. In this century, the innovative composer and theorist Arnold Schoenberg declared the integrity of nontonal (i.e., atonal) music, while also proclaiming that there was still plenty of good music waiting to be written in the key of C.

Further Reading and Listening

General Histories

Lang, Paul Henry. *Music in Western Civilization.* New York: W. W. Norton, 1941.

Pauly, Reinhard G. *Music in the Classic Period.* New Jersey: Prentice Hall, 1965.

Rosen, Charles. *The Classical Style.* New York: W.W. Norton, 1972.

Schonberg, Harold. *Lives of the Great Composers.* New York: W. W. Norton, 1981.

Swafford, Jan. *The Vintage Guide to Classical Music.* New York: Vintage/Knopf, 1992.

Writings on Mozart

Deutsch, Otto Erich. *Mozart, a Documentary Biography*. Stanford: Stanford University Press, 1965.

Einstein, Alfred. *Mozart, The Man and His Music*. New York: Oxford University Press, 1945.

Girdlestone, Cuthbert M. *Mozart and His Piano Concertos*. Oklahoma: University of Oklahoma Press, 1952.

Landon, H.C. Robbins. *Mozart, the Golden Years*. New York: Schirmer, 1989.

————. *Mozart's Last Year*. New York: Schirmer, 1988.

Zaslaw, Neal and Cowdey, William (ed.). *The Compleat Mozart*, New York: W. W. Norton, 1990.

A Selective Mozart Discography

Piano Concertos Nos. 22 (K. 482) and **24** (K. 491). It's not enough to have just one disc of the piano concertos, and this one pairs two truly extraordinary works, full of gorgeous wind scoring; Murray Perahia plays and conducts eloquently. Sony MK 42242.

Così fan tutte (K. 589). Performed in the elegant setting of Sweden's eighteenth-century Drottningholm Theater, with marvelous ensemble singing. L'Oiseau Lyre 441-316-2/3/4.

Mass in C minor (K. 427). Powerful choral writing and sublime writing for soprano soloist—the wonderful Sylvia McNair in this John Eliot Gardiner reading. Philips 420-210-2.

Quartets Nos. 17 (K. 458) and ***19*** (K. 465). Both date from the same time as the Concertos. One is the joyous *Hunt* Quartet; the other, the *Dissonant* Quartet with its mysterious slow introduction in strong, beautifully controlled performances by the Alban Berg Quartet. Teldec 2202-43037.

Quintets in C (K. 515) and ***G minor*** (K. 516). Chamber music for five strings never got more profound than these extraordinary, rich works, played with silk and steel by the Tokyo Quartet with Pinchas Zukerman as the extra violist. RCA 09026-60940.

Serenades for Winds in B-flat (K. 361) and ***C minor*** (K. 388). Profound works despite their lightweight connotation; the B-flat is the work in which Salieri of *Amadeus* hears "a voice of God," and he's right this once. Colin Davis conducts the winds of his Bavarian State Radio Orchestra. RCA 09026-60673.

Sinfonia Concertante for Violin and Viola (K. 364) and ***for Winds*** (K. 297b). Mozart comes into his expressive maturity in the wondrous violin/viola work; the wind sinfonia, of dubious parentage, shows the hands of other editors, but there are pretty moments in this performance by Orpheus, a conductorless chamber orchestra. Deutsche Grammophon 429-784-2.

Sonatas for Piano. Anthony Newman holds his cult following as one of the "authentic instrument" pioneers. His traversal, on four discs, is greatly enhanced by the sound of his piano. Newport Classic 60121/4.

Symphonies Nos. 36 in C (K. 425, "Linz") and ***38 in D*** (K. 504, "Prague"). Eloquent music created for cities of sophisticated taste, elegantly played by the Prague Chamber Orchestra under Charles Mackerras. Telarc 60148.

The Mozart Edition. To celebrate the 1991 bicentennial of Mozart's death, Philips issued virtually every note from his pen, taking up 181 mid-priced compact discs in forty-five separate boxes—all the piano concertos in one twelve-disc box, all the masses in a nine-disc box, etc. The performances tend to be superb, emphatically so in the case of Alfred Brendel's piano concertos, Mitsuko Uchida's piano sonatas, and the symphonies under Neville Marriner. The boxes are sold separately; someday, the individual discs may be as well. Nobody is going to claim absolute superiority for every performance, but the quality is remarkably high. One could, in other words, do worse. Philips 422-501/422-3545.

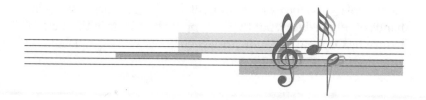